Amy Lowell Among
Her Contemporaries

Amy Lowell Among Her Contemporaries

Carl Rollyson

ASJA Press
New York   Bloomington

Amy Lowell Among Her Contemporaries

Copyright © 2009 by Carl Rollyson

All rights reserved. No part of this book may be used or reproduced by any means, graphic, electronic, or mechanical, including photocopying, recording, taping or by any information storage retrieval system without the written permission of the publisher except in the case of brief quotations embodied in critical articles and reviews.

The views expressed in this work are solely those of the author and do not necessarily reflect the views of the publisher, and the publisher hereby disclaims any responsibility for them.

ASJA Press
an imprint of iUniverse, Inc.

iUniverse books may be ordered through booksellers or by contacting:

iUniverse
1663 Liberty Drive
Bloomington, IN 47403
www.iuniverse.com
1-800-Authors (1-800-288-4677)

Because of the dynamic nature of the Internet, any Web addresses or links contained in this book may have changed since publication and may no longer be valid.

ISBN: 978-1-4502-0080-6 (sc)

Printed in the United States of America

iUniverse rev. date: 12/28/2009

BY CARL ROLLYSON

Biographies

Marilyn Monroe: A Life of the Actress
Lillian Hellman: Her Legend and Her Legacy
Beautiful Exile: The Life of Martha Gellhorn
The Lives of Norman Mailer
Rebecca West: A Saga of the Century
Pablo Picasso
Susan Sontag: The Making of an Icon (with Lisa Paddock)
Marie Curie: Honesty in Science
To Be A Woman: The Life of Jill Craigie
A Private Life of Michael Foot (forthcoming)

On Biography

Adventures of an Outlaw: A Biographer at Work (forthcoming)
Biography: An Annotated Bibliography
Reading Biography
Essays in Biography
A Higher Form of Cannibalism? Adventures in the Art and Politics of Biography
British Biography: A Reader
Biography Before Boswell: A Reader
Female Icons: Marilyn Monroe to Susan Sontag
Lives of the Novelists
Biography: A User's Guide

Literary Criticism

Uses of the Past in the Novels of William Faulkner
The Literary Legacy of Rebecca West
Rebecca West and the God That Failed: Essays
Reading Susan Sontag

Film Criticism

Documentary Film: A Primer
Documentary Film: Contexts and Criticism

Interviews

In Their Own Voices: Teenage Refugees from Eastern Europe Speak Out

Reference Works

Herman Melville A to Z (with Lisa Paddock)
The Brontës A to Z (with Lisa Paddock)
The Facts on File Encyclopedia of American Literature, Volume 3: The Modern Period and Postmodern Period From 1915
Where America Stands: What Americans Think and Need to Know About Today's Most Critical Issues (with Michael Golay)

Genealogy

*A Student's Guide to Polish-American Genealogy (*with Lisa Paddock*)*
A Student's Guide to Scandinavian-American Genealogy (with Lisa Paddock*)*

Editor

Critical Survey of Drama, Second Revised Edition
Critical Survey of Long Fiction, Second Revised Edition
Notable British Novelists
Notable American Novelists
Critical Survey of Mystery and Detective Fiction, Second Revised Edition

Contents

	Preface	ix
1	The Absence of Amy Lowell	1
2	A Tale of a Tub: Amy Lowell and Ezra Pound	9
3	"A Sort of Congenital Understanding": Amy Lowell and D. H. Lawrence	38
4	Wearing Well: Amy Lowell and Robert Frost	67
5	The Big Blue Wave: Amy Lowell and Florence Ayscough	82
6	Remembering Amy Lowell	101
7	Brief Portraits, Cameos, Walk-ons	157
	Endnotes	167
	Appendix A: Imagists	175
	Appendix B: Amy Lowell: Selected Poetry	187

Preface

An alternative title for this volume might be "Justice to Amy Lowell." Although she has been the subject of several biographies, her image and reputation seemed fixed in the biographies and memoirs of others. As a result, Lowell appears almost exclusively through the perceptions of her male biographers and their subjects. A tempting target—as I explain in "The Absence of Amy Lowell"--she is often skewered, or at the very least distorted by insensitive writers who never seem to pause and question the stories about her. In this series of essays, beginning with a look at how her own biographers have behaved, I have tried to re-conceive the familiar anecdotes and episodes, circling back again and again to certain incidents and contretemps, as the point of view shifts from one writer to another.[1]

As a kind of coda to my quarrel with biographers is an essay, "Remembering Amy Lowell," in which I assess the varying degrees to which the memoirs of her present a credible person and poet.

I have not paused to define in any great detail terms such as Imagism, although I've included an essay on the Imagists in an appendix as well as the full texts of the poems discussed in this book. These appendices provide a context for the discussion of Lowell and her contemporaries and serve, I hope, as an inviting introduction to her work.

1

The Absence of Amy Lowell

When Amy Lowell died in 1925 at the age of 51, she was at the height of her fame. Her two-volume biography of John Keats, published in the last year of her life, had been greeted in this country with almost universal acclaim. She was the premier platform performer among her generation of poets.

In 1926, Lowell's posthumous volume of verse, *What's O'Clock,* was awarded a Pulitzer Prize. She had remained in the public eye ever since the publication of her second book. *Sword Blades and Poppy Seed* (1914). She had wrested the Imagist movement away from Ezra Pound, producing three best-selling anthologies of Imagist verse while publishing a book of her own poetry nearly every year. Pound retaliated, calling her appropriation "Amygism."

The pugnacious Lowell dominated the poetry scene in every sense of the word, supporting journals like *Poetry* and *The Little Review.,* and publishing pronunciamentos about the "new poetry." Standing only five feet tall and weighing as much as 250 pounds, she made good copy: The sister of Harvard's president, she smoked cigars and cursed.

She lived on the family estate in Brookline, Massachusetts, where her seven rambunctious sheep dogs terrorized her guests. She wore a pince nez that made her look—so one biographer thought—like Theodore Roosevelt. She was even known to say "Bully!"

Lowell traveled in a maroon Pierce Arrow, which she shipped to England in 1914 when she decided to look up Pound and seize her piece of the poetry action in London. Pound wanted her monetary support but scorned her verse. When she chose not to play by his rules, he mocked her, parading around a party she was hosting with a tin bathtub on his head—his way of ridiculing her bath poem, written in her patented polyphonic prose:

> Little spots of sunshine lie on the surface of the water and dance, dance, and their reflections wobble deliciously over the ceiling; a stir of my finger sets them whirring, reeling. I move a foot, and the planes of light in the water jar. I lie back and laugh, and let the green-white water, the sun-flawed beryl water, flow over me. The day is almost too bright to bear, the green water covers me from the too bright day. I will lie here awhile and play with the water and the sun spots.

Reading this dithyramb to the Poetry Society of America, Lowell caused an uproar. This was not poetry at all, the conservative membership protested. Another account of this episode mentions titters, as Society members envisioned the elephantine poet at her ablutions—or rather her profanation of what a dignified poet ought to perform.

Lowell went on lecture tours the way rock bands roll from town to town today, with an entourage, a suite at the best hotel, and a gathering of reporters awaiting her latest outrage. On the lecture platform, she would read a poem and then pause, looking out at her audience: "Well, hiss or applaud! But do something!" Almost always she got an ovation—and some hisses. At receptions and dinner parties, she was carefully watched. When would she light up? She seldom disappointed, although her favored stogie was, in fact, a small brown panatela and not the big black cigars featured in the more sensational reports.

Other women poets—chiefly Elinor Wylie and Edna St. Vincent Millay—also commanded press attention, but none had Amy Lowell's authority. Publishers deferred to her contractual terms. D. H. Lawrence, Richard Aldington, H. D., and others depended on her largesse and her business sense. She was Poetry, Inc. Today she would be, of course, Poetry.com. T. S. Eliot called her the "demon saleswoman" of modern poetry. Academic critics such as John Livingston Lowes deemed her one of the masters of the sensuous image in English poetry. She helped make the reputations of Edwin Arlington Robinson and Robert Frost.

Of course, Lowell had her detractors, but their views were rarely reflected in reviews of her books. As Norman Mailer said of Marilyn Monroe—Lowell had crashed through a publicity barrier, which meant that no matter what kind of press she got, it all accrued to her benefit. Although she came from a wealthy and staunchly capitalist family and called herself "the last of the barons," it was not her politics but her poetics that captured the public imagination. She was for free verse, or what she called "cadenced verse." Although she would produce sonnets and other sorts of poems with rhyme schemes, she was celebrated for lines of uneven length, a bold, informal voice, and bright, colorful sensory imagery. Lowell was all surface, her grumbling dissenters alleged, but she always seemed to carry the day by switching modes—from grand historical narratives, to hokkus, to lyrics, to polyphonic prose, to books about contemporary poetry that read as though she had just left the lecture platform to address you, the common reader.

It is not surprising, then, that her enemies—never able to get much traction during her lifetime—should pounce just as soon as the energetic Lowell dropped dead from a stroke. The urge to cut this incubus down to size was irresistible. Clement Wood, a poet and critic who had feuded with Lowell, was first up in 1926, producing a biography systematically dismantling Lowell's reputation as a poet and critic.[2] Lowell had been prolific and prolix, producing in a fifteen-year span an immense and uneven variety of verse and prose that made her an easy target for tendentious criticism. Wood's verdict, in short, was that Lowell was no poet at all. He skirted her lesbianism with references to the "Sapphic fragments" of a "singer of Lesbos." He employed what he called the "new psychology" to suggest her work was wish fulfillment, the product of a desire to be accepted. Lowell's need was pathological. Wood implied, because of her obesity—a word he never used, referring instead to her "immense physique." Wood favored sarcasm, concluding, "All the Harvard pundits and all the claquing men can't set Miss Lowell on a pedestal again." He was chaffing John Livingston Lowes, chair of Harvard's English department, and countless critics who had reviewed her writing positively.

Lowell's next biographer, S. Foster Damon, produced a monumental biography in 1935, noting that Wood's snide attack had not been widely reviewed or credited, but the damage had been done—in part because Wood had played off the epithets of critics like Witter Byner, who had dubbed Lowell the "hippopoetess," a term Ezra Pound also took up as a way of conflating the person with the poet. Damon, a member of Lowell's inner circle, restored her dignity by detailing her heroic dedication to her writing and to the cause of poetry, but he also unwittingly played Wood's hand by emphasizing the "triumph of the spirit over the tragedy of the body." Poetry, in other words, is what Lowell could do instead of living a full, "normal" life. Damon meant his words as a tribute, but because he did not tell the complete story of Lowell's love life and her working days, he could not recover for readers the Amy Lowell he knew.

Damon's plight raises two issues that plague Lowell biography. Lowell's lover and constant companion, Ada Dwyer Russell, destroyed their letters at Lowell's request. As unfortunate was Lowell's directive to her secretaries that they destroy the drafts of her work each day. Damon could have partly rectified this enormous loss had he candidly described the intimacy between "Peter" (Lowell's nickname for Ada) and the poet. But Russell, who had worked closely with the poet, was also Lowell's executor. Russell lived until 1952, resisting all requests to tell the story of her relationship with Lowell, and thus depriving readers not merely of a love story but of an insight into the poetic process.

Damon's reticence made it all too easy for Wood's virulent version of Lowell to metastasize in Horace Gregory's hostile *Amy Lowell: Portrait of the Poet in Her Time* (1958). Employing Wood's vulgar Freudianism, Gregory sketched a view of a masculinized woman who used her bulk as a defense against a hurtful world. Gregory seemed to have no idea that Russell and Lowell had been lovers, although the evidence was rather plain to see, eventually emerging in Jean Gould's *Amy: The World of Amy Lowell and the Imagist Movement* (1975). Relying on critics such as Glenn Richard Ruihley, who published in 1957 an edition of Lowell's poetry that emphasized her stunning love poetry, as well as on fresh interviews with Lowell's surviving family and friends, Gould began the work of restoring the person and poet to her full humanity and range. But Gould was unwilling to confront the implications of Lowell's subtler poems, in which she carefully disrobed for the world. Gould balked at going "half-way with poets" and feeling "the thing you're out to find," as Lowell wrote in one of her last poems. Gould quoted but did not explore the subtext of her subject's passionate poetry.

Enter C. David Heymann with *American Aristocracy: The Lives and Times of James Russell, Amy, and Robert Lowell* (1980), determined to drag Lowell back to Gregory's procrustean bed. Heymann cut and pasted the work of Lowell's previous biographers, quoted a few published memoirs, and delivered a breezy reprise of the standard brief against Amy Lowell, beginning with Louis Untermeyer's devastating verdict: "Amy Lowell had a genius for everything except the thing she wanted most: permanence as a poet." Heymann pictures Lowell as "naive, unknowing, and innocent," pronouncing her brashness a cover for a "gigantic inferiority complex" and a "troubled psyche." He delivers his judgments with ex cathedra certainty: "The need to make a kind of technicolor charade of her life was one way of making up for its essential emptiness." And he denies her precisely what recent critics, male and female, have found most valuable in her verse: a deep understanding of love. Instead, he indulges in that most odious of biographical practices: presenting lack of evidence as somehow an occasion for insisting on the validity of what he cannot know. Thus he argues that in the first stanza of Lowell's signature poem "Patterns," "she must have had herself in mind" protesting against "Puritan inhibitions and society's repressive conventions." But Lowell seemed remarkably well adjusted, adroitly negotiating both the high society world of her family and the rarified precincts of poets. It is odd that her aplomb should so often be mistaken for ingenuousness, as if she did not know enough to be embarrassed by her bulk and her fortune. To be sure, she had her share of self-doubt, but I cannot help but think her air of self-containment nettled those like Pound and Eliot who could find no place for her in the narrative of modernism. Better to think of her as an amateur, a lady poet, and a clubwoman. Hence Heymann guywires her to "Miss Lowell" and "Amy," whereas Pound is never Ezra and Untermeyer is never Mr. Untermeyer.

Heymann calls Lowell's erotic poems "androgynous," born of a close friendship with Ada that was not "necessarily sexual in nature." Why is he so wary of discussing Lowell's sexuality when he is so confident about other aspects of her inner life? It seems that he could not resist joining a long line of male critics who could not envision the body of Amy Lowell in the act of love. Although she did sometimes express anguish and even disgust about her figure ("Look at me," she once said, "I'm a disease"), Lowell wrote poetry that celebrated the bodies of herself, her lover, and other women. Indeed, she often lectured about Whitman and shared his amative nature. Far from suffering from some void in her life, Lowell positively embraced her sexuality.

Modernists like William Carlos Williams could not abide a poet like Lowell, a conservative who refused to apologize for her wealth. Like Pound, he wrote her letters telling her off while asking her for money. Heymann thought it odd that Lowell did not make common cause with feminists given her own "liberated" relationship with Ada Dwyer. That he did not see that he has contradicted himself, providing Lowell with an erotic experience he had previously denied her, is just another index of his un-willingness to see the person and the poet.

Critics like Lillian Faderman and Melissa Bradshaw and poets like Honor Moore, who edited *Amy Lowell: Selected Poems* (The Library of America, 2004), have since become attuned to her bold eroticism, a force that beautifully binds the physical and spiritual, as in these lines from "Absence," Lowell's love poem to Ada Russell:

> My cup is empty to-night.
> Cold and dry are its sides ....
> But the cup of the heart is still.
> And cold, and empty.
> When you come it brims
> Red and trembling with blood.
> Heart's blood for your drinking;
> To fill your mouth with love
> And the bitter-sweet taste of a soul.

These were the lines D. H. Lawrence extolled when he expressed his affinity with Lowell, which Lowell herself acknowledged when she quoted back to him his praise for her "insistence on *things*. My things are always, to my mind, more than themselves."

She begins with a cup that is always a cup but is also her heart and then her mouth, just as her lover's coming is both a return and a climax; the literal, the sexual, and the symbolic merge.

Of even greater importance, however, are poems like "The Onlooker" (first published in the *Saturday Review of Literature*, February 1925), which fuses the personal with the historical, espying in an erotic encounter the fate of a civilization:

> Suppose I plant you
> Like wide-eyed Helen
> On the battlements
> Of weary Troy,
> Clutching the parapet with desperate hands.
> She, too, gazes at a battlefield
> Where bright vermillion plumes and metal whiteness
> Shock and sparkle and go down with groans.
> Her glances strike the rocking battle.
> Again—again—
> Recoiling from it
> Like baffled spear-heads fallen from a brazen shield.
> The ancients at her elbow counsel patience
> and contingencies;
> Such to a woman stretched upon a bed of battle.
> Who bargained for this only in the whispering arras
> Enclosed about a midnight of enchantment.

This Amy Lowell is akin to Constantine Cavafy or Zbigniew Herbert in her reverie over a historic moment, and the conceit that she was no poet seems palpably put-on, part of a master narrative that ought to be annihilated once and for all.

2

A Tale of a Tub: Amy Lowell and Ezra Pound

When I decided to embark on a biography of Amy Lowell, a fellow biographer wondered how I would get on with such an unsympathetic character. I was not surprised at the comment, understanding that Amy Lowell seemed a blustering, bullying figure whose poetry no longer commanded that much respect and whose personality therefore seemed all the more distasteful. We forgive our poets their petty failings so long as they perform well. But I thought Lowell was a better poet than the current cant about her suggested, and, anyway, I took umbrage on my subject's behalf. Biographers do not have to love their subjects—except as subjects, fascinating figures for a biographical narrative. I also suspected that the case against Lowell could be taken apart once I examined her relations with her contemporaries. Because of her involvement with Ezra Pound, one of the presiding modernist poets, I presumed that her side of the story had been discounted. So I went looking for scenes from Amy Lowell's life that ought to be viewed afresh. My bias, I am bound to confess, arose out of a determination to do justice to Amy Lowell.

I intend to write this chapter in the order of my reading to show how I slowly came to certain conclusions about what I shall call the bathtub scene. In doing so, I hope to reveal the shiftings of interpretation in my sources and in my reactions to those sources. Thus I may be able to convey how a biographer sets about assembling his narrative, discarding or modifying impressions while aiming at a well-rounded, synoptic account. In part, I also want to demonstrate that how we come to view a subject is, in part, influenced by the sequence of research, which is a constant re-evaluation of first impressions and prejudices.

So what happened between Amy Lowell and Ezra Pound? They had two important encounters—in the spring of 1913 and then in the late summer of 1914. When Lowell first met Pound, she was seeking guidance. She had published one volume of verse, *A Dome of Many-Coloured Glass* (1912), inspired by her saturation in romantic poetry. Some of this work had been written as early as 1903, and most of it represented an apprenticeship in poetry, born of a desire to excel but also of a despair that she would ever make the grade as a poet. Because she later acquired a reputation as a formidable figure, a bulky 240-pounder who knew how to throw around her influence as a member of the New England aristocracy, many commentators have assumed that she lacked self-awareness, let alone humility. No one, critics have supposed, could publish a book so derivative and so undistinguished except a spoiled, self-regarding wealthy woman used to the privileges accorded to a long line of Lowells who had dominated Boston's commercial and literary precincts.

But *A Dome of Many-Coloured Glass* is not a work of vanity. On the contrary, it is a courageous effort to expose her sensibility and to discover just what the world outside of her native Brookline made of her desire to write. The book was in a curious way a confession of failure—one that is sometimes uttered through a persona but often through a voice that seems Lowell's own. After a decade of writing mainly for herself, Lowell no longer shielded herself from the world at large. She wanted to *know* where she stood, and only through publication can a writer brave a verdict.

She also came as a kind of supplicant to the altar of poetry. Indeed the first poem of her collection, "Before the Altar," features a disconsolate figure who refers to the "gifts I have not brought." The "poet's dreams" have come to naught, "hopes turning quick to fears." This failure of nerve is personal, with certain poems expressing her keen loneliness and sense of incompleteness: "never shall I be fulfilled by love," the speaker of "A Fairy Tale" laments. So distraught is her mood in "The Starling" that she yearns "to be some other person for a day."

Many of the poems are not merely an expression of failure; the poems themselves are failures. It is almost as if Lowell sought public humiliation, a confrontation with the worst that could be said about her work. *A Dome of Many-Coloured Glass* is certainly not a work of self-delusion.

And yet Lowell's first book contains pieces—only a few—that show promise. Would anyone notice? Few did. The reviews were lukewarm. Even so, Lowell did not give up, no matter how she much she rued the "poor restless soul" that appears in "The Starling." She read Harriet Monroe's *Poetry*, finding in Ezra Pound's article about Imagism a credo she could identify as her own. Again, commentators have puzzled over her declaration that she was an Imagist when *A Dome of Many-Coloured Glass*, they claim, lacked the discipline, precise observation, and devotion to what William Carlos Williams later called, "no ideas but in things."

Richard Benvenuto, one of Lowell's most discerning critics, wonders if these skeptics actually read Lowell with any care. Take, for example, "The Green Bowl." The first three lines exemplify the cadenced free verse she would later champion:

> This little bowl is like a mossy pool
> In a Spring wood, where dogtooth violets grow
> Nodding in chequered sunshine of the trees;

The subtle rhyming of bowl and grow, the liquid l sounds and the sibilance of the s sounds, provide a pictorial and musical composition that unites the worlds of art and nature. The sounds of the words merge and confer a coherence on one another.

In the next three lines, Lowell emerges as a modern poet adapting the formal grandeur of her beloved Keats's "Ode on a Grecian Urn," to a far more relaxed musing on art's extension of nature's impact on human consciousness:

> A quiet place, still, with the sound of birds,
> Where, though unseen, is heard the endless song
> And murmur of the never resting sea.

The quiet place is the bowl, which is "still," but also the mossy pool, the remembered nature scene that is also part of the artist's anticipation of seasonal change that is evoked in the next line (see below). The shaping of the bowl/cup becomes a sacramental act, a devotion to life itself in the shape of a work of art that both mimics and cherishes nature even as it expresses the human defilement of what it loves:

> 'T was winter, Roger, when you made this cup,
> But coming Spring guided your hand
> And round the edge you fashioned young green leaves,
> A proper chalice made to hold the shy
> And little flowers of the woods. And here
> They will forget their sad uprooting, lost
> In pleasure that this circle of bright leaves
> Should be their setting; once more they will dream
> They hear winds wandering through lofty trees
> And see the sun smiling through the leaves.

If the ending seems forced and trite--shouldn't the poet close with the "shy and little flowers of the woods"?--the image works, even with the word "shy," since dogtooth violets do naturally bend their yellow leaves toward the ground in a reticent posture. The rest of the poem is overstatement. The notion that art somehow compensates for nature's loss seems didactic--the kind of supererogatory "moral" that 19th century poets appended to their poems.

This is to say that Lowell was half-way to Imagism without realizing it—or rather, she realized it as soon as she read Pound. He represented a new century and the new mode of poetry she could seek only by writing herself out of the old forms without quite understanding how to supercede them.

By not accounting for the transition Lowell was attempting in a poem like "The Green Bowl," her arrival in London to accost Pound seems only an expression of a domineering personality. Thus John Tytell, *Ezra Pound: The Solitary Volcano*, introduces her via Harriet Monroe's comment on Lowell's "ponderous regal air" and "imperious ambition for a literary career." To be sure, Monroe had a point, but not one that gets at the nub of Lowell's motivation. Thus she is forced to labor under Tytell's bias when he reports Richard Aldington's verdict on *A Dome of Many-Coloured Glass*: "fruity and facile."

Lowell invites Pound to her hotel suite and reads him poems, which he calls "saccharine." But he is diplomatic, realizing that Lowell's wealth could fund his aesthetic projects. He is "determined to convert her to free verse and Imagism." He introduces her to Ford Madox Ford and William Butler Yeats. At dinner he reads her two of his poems, "The Seafarer" and "Sestina: Altaforte" "as a demonstration of the new poetry." But Tytell calls the poems old in form and diction—"he himself was not yet clear about what direction the new could take."

So Lowell arrives looking for guidance but realizes that Pound, for all his bravado, is still at sea himself. Remember, this is early Pound, the tyro with the twirling cane, goatee, and flowing cape. Although Lowell is often pictured as the overbearing one, it is Pound who makes her nervous. Tytell adds this little bit for color, not realizing what he is reporting: She lights one of her cigars while Pound reads, admitting they are "good for her nerves." But Tytell writes as though she has no nerves. Instead he relies on Lowell's letter to Harriet Monroe, describing Pound as charming and full of youthful enthusiasm: ""a very thin-skinned and sensitive personality opening out like a flower in a sympathetic circle, and I should imagine shutting up like a clam in an alien atmosphere. . . ." In her letter, Lowell sounds commanding, a confident judge of character, who adds: "That he will outgrow some of his theories, I feel sure. . . . I think the chip-on-the-shoulder attitude will disappear in time." She was eleven years older than Pound, which accounts for her perspective. But consider also that her letter to Monroe asserts mastery over a confrontation that in all likelihood rattled her. No one in her experience had talked about poetry with Pound's mania and aplomb. His ambition for poetry was as daunting as it was exhilarating.

But Tytell has before him only the image of the dominatrix returning for a second go at Pound in the eve of World War I:

> Amy Lowell steamed back to London complete with her retinue of maids, her liveried chauffeur, and her maroon limousine—like a good American, she went nowhere without her own automobile. . . . determined to save the world with poetry, and she felt she had some credentials. Actually she had very little of a self-critical faculty. Arguing with her, Carl Sandburg observed, was like struggling with a "great blue wave."

I'm sure Lowell thought as much of Sandburg. Tytell does not bother to reflect that how Amy traveled did not necessarily express the poet within. He makes her seem not merely devoid of introspection but also of good sense—a naïve American like Woodrow Wilson saving the world not for democracy but for poetry. Tytell supposes that Lowell could not argue with herself and that she could bring to England only the mental equipment of the ugly American.

Tytell treats the dinner Lowell hosted for Pound and his fellow Imagists: Aldington, H. D., John Cournos, R. W. Flint, Allen Upward, and John Gould Fletcher as her bid to turn the tables on Pound, replacing him as the center of attention. Her behavior seems presumptuous since she was just beginning to write the poetry that would fill her second volume, *Sword Blades and Poppy Seed* (1914), a marked advance over earlier work. But this negative view of Lowell can be sustained only if other possibilities are not canvassed. As a woman of wealth, she could afford to draw talent around her—not for the purpose of showing off or of commandeering Pound's group but to learn from it, to open herself all at once to these different voices that would never be heard so long as Pound controlled those one-on-one meetings that Lowell had puffed her way through.

But treating everyone to a meal invites suspicion and the desire to bite the hand that feeds one. Thus Tytell relies on John Cournos's recollection of an "undercurrent of hostility and condescension toward Lowell." Then Allen Upward read from Lowell's poem, "In a Garden," which Pound had chosen for his anthology, *Des Imagistes* (1914). Identifying Lowell with the poem's speaker, Cournos suggested that Upward pictured her bathing in a moonlit garden in "a way to perturb and vex her puritanic soul." I read this phrase several times wondering why Tytell put such store in it. Certainly, Lowell was the daughter of Puritan New England, but she was already living with her lover Ada Russell, and nothing about Lowell from adolescence onward seems the least puritanical. In short, Cournos was projecting a meaning into the scene that just seems flat wrong.

While I puzzle over Tytell's incoherent account, he rushes to wrap up the episode: Pound has left the dinner and returned with "a circular tub he had found in an adjoining room and placed it in front of Amy Lowell, announcing that *Les Imagistes* were about to be succeeded by *Les Nagistes*. Upward and Pound had conspired to embarrass Amy Lowell; it was a crude baptism in the politics of poetry." To be sure, Pound was crude, but was his caper intended to do anything more than embarrass Lowell? And what was her reaction? And what did the rest of the group make of it?

Tytell leans on Aldington's explanation: Lowell wanted an expanded edition of a second Imagist anthology with work chosen by the poets themselves instead of edited by Pound. "With some reason Pound was afraid of Amy Lowell's taste," Tytell observes. Her desire to democratize the selection process would sacrifice standards and would result in "splay-footed and sentimental" work. Aldington said that Amy Lowell's visit was Pound's "Boston Tea Party, the dethroning of the Imagist Duce and the ending of his 'capricious censorship.'" Tytell concludes that Pound's comments were "high-handed and lofty" and reports that R. W. Flint told Pound, "You have not been a good comrade."

Tytell notes that the three anthologies Lowell shepherded to publication popularized Imagism, helped H. D.'s reputation, but also "provoked lots of negative comment." He cites criticism by important writes such Conrad Aiken and May Sinclair. Tytell believes Imagism had been "watered down and compromised."

Tytell does not countenance that Imagism and the work of its poets would have been much slower to develop without Lowell's intervention. And he does not wonder why, in addition to her money, Lowell succeeded in arousing such loyalty. In part, she prevailed because she was the anti-Pound and promoted the feeling that these poets could work for a common good without sacrificing their individual styles. She was tolerant, and encouraged diversity. And unlike Pound, she was still searching for her own standards, still finding herself as a poet. It took a certain courage to submit herself to the critiques of others, especially Aldington and Lawrence, who may have wanted to placate her but who also exercised a modicum of honesty about her own work in order to preserve the integrity of their own. Above all, her encouragement was such a relief from the dictatorial, prescriptive Pound.

Noel Stock, *The Life of Ezra Pound*, parallels Tytell, but adds this detail about how Lowell's physical appearance was made the focal point of the bathtub scene: "Upward and several others present made fun of Miss Lowell's stoutness and drew attention to the line, 'not in the water, but you in your whiteness, bathing.'" In this version, everyone piles on, which seems doubtful, since this is the group that formed the nucleus of her Imagist anthologies. Even more than Tytell, Stock cannot see beyond (or around) Lowell's bulk and her fortune: "Looking at the quarrel now it is clear that in the matter of literary principle Pound was in the right." But Stock goes on to cite a Lowell letter questioning Pound's motives and concludes: "it seems likely that money or the manner in which Miss Lowell chose to spend her money entered into their quarrel." Pound saw Lowell primarily as a money bag, hoping she would fund various projects, including his work on *The Egoist*. She did not choose to spend her money on Pound. But that she had the money in the first place, of course, is what made her a mark for Pound's schemes.

Not surprisingly, S. Foster Damon, Lowell's loyal friend and authorized biographer presents a sympathetic portrayal of her contretemps with Pound. He emphasizes her disappointment over the tepid reception of *A Dome of Many-Coloured Glass* and her avid desire to absorb the new doctrines of the Imagists. London appeals to Lowell because it is an antidote to "uncentralized America." But she also has something to offer the Imagists: a determination to get them published in the U. S., which is an appealing gambit to poets who find their work ignored or even abused in England.

Soon, however, John Gould Fletcher, Pound'a arch-opponent is telling her "of all things on earth, the most abominable was the London literary clique, with its external politeness and internal jealousies and underground tactics." Thus Damon sets the scene: the straightforward Lowell enters an atmosphere thick with intrigue and betrayal. Yet other than noting Ford Madox Ford's hostility to Lowell, Damon refrains from the dramatics of other accounts: no bathtub, no ridiculing of Lowell's poem, "In A Garden." Indeed, Damon insists that Lowell's dinner with the Imagists was quite jolly, with Upward giving "a particularly happy speech."

Most accounts ignore Ada Russell, who accompanied Lowell to London and was present at the bathtub scene. Damon mentions Russell without explaining how her presence affected the group.[3] At the very least, Russell who served as lover, companion, and private secretary, bolstered Lowell and, I suspect, contributed to the confidence and calm Lowell exhibited at the dinner. What did the Imagists make of this couple? Did they ignore Russell? That is hard to believe given the poise the experienced stage actress was remembered for. She was Lowell's better half—her guardian angel. And it is a grievous loss to Lowell biography that her participation in this key moment in Lowell's development as poet and impresario of Imagism has not even been acknowledged by Pound's or Lowell's biographers, so obsessed with the clashing of Pound's and Lowell's egos. The truth is that what has not been written about this conflict is far more important than what the few eyewitnesses have selectively reported.

Damon seeks to show that Lowell harbored no resentment in spite of Pound's rough handling of her: "In spite of the subsequent feud, she always insisted on Pound's ability to stimulate." This is certainly born out by Lowell's letters about Pound. As Damon also notes, until her London visits, Lowell had been working in isolation, which meant she had not subjected herself to the kind of first-rate commentary available in London:

> The *Imagiste* criticism consequently was opening the gates of creation. The mild melancholy of *Domes* melted away instantly as the gusto of reality came within her hand. . . . [T[hey rewrote her old poems before her eyes, underscoring *clichés* (Ezra's word) and heaving them out; compressing; making more visible; brooming away Victorian cobwebs; reducing morals to implications; breaking up stiff lines, then reassembling them in any number of different ways, to choose the one with the best cadence; in general, cleaning up "literature" and concentrating on reality.

Lowell would later show Pound her poem about their controversy. In "Astigmatism," a highly cultivated poet with an elaborately beautiful walking cane uses it to knock off the heads of daisies, irises, dahlias—all because they are not roses (his notion of supreme perfection and beauty). In Lowell's view, Pound could not see and did not know how to preserve the everyday beauty that she celebrated in her work. As she remarked in *A Critical Fable*: "Pound was born in an orchard, but his/trees have the rust." Even worse, he could see art only in terms of a very narrowly defined ideal. Even as he saw her as indiscriminate, she saw him as too rarified. His ideal ultimately led to death and destruction. She admired his work but thought poetry per se suffered because of his dogmatic principles.

Jean Gould, *Amy: The World of Amy Lowell and the Imagist Movement*, concentrates on the mystique Pound accorded poetry. In Gould's view, Lowell went to London because

Pound was so secretive about Imagism, declaring it was not for the general public.

Gould adds a few, suspect details to the tub tale, reporting that when Lowell asks Pound about Imagism, he leaves the room at the Dieudonne restaurant and returns shortly with "an old fashioned tin tub on his head in caricature of a helmet of some knight-errant. He produced hilarious laughter, in which Amy joined, but hers was a hard and a hurt laugh." How does Gould know the laugh was hard and hurt? The very phrasing of Lowell's response owes more to the biographer's desire to create a scene than to what Lowell might actually have expressed. And again, what Pound meant by his antics baffles the biographer. Gould does not care to speculate, so I will: Was Pound implying that Lowell was tilting at windmills? Was he dramatizing her Quixotism? Was he demonstrating that what he had dubbed *Imagisme* was old hat? Or simply that he, Pound, had to be the cynosure of all eyes? At the very least, his foolery had the effect of diverting any serious discussion.

Several critics have noted Horace Gregory's animus toward Lowell. In *Amy Lowell: Portrait of the Poet in Her Time*, he introduces her as a blunderbuss: "Without being aware of her intrusion (since she was welcomed) and without clear knowledge of what being a member of Pound's circle implied, Amy Lowell entered the list of *Imagistes*. She was a self-appointed member of the group." She is wealthy and regal, and this accounts for her impact on the Imagists who join her. She is also "maternal," and that one word is enough for Gregory to explain why Richard Aldington, then an impressionable 20, should side with Lowell.

Gregory's interpretation of the bathtub scene: "impertinent Vorticism,[4] too much drink, Bohemianism, disrespect for the hostess—but all signs pointed toward a further coolness between Amy Lowell and Ezra Pound. In Ezra Pound's presence, Amy Lowell was never allowed to be the center of attention." Because

Gregory believes Lowell is upset that Pound has upstaged her, he suggests "Astigmatism" is not about the differences between Lowell and Pound regarding poetry but rather an example of pique, even though the poem's refrain, "Peace be with you, Brother," suggests Lowell's desire not to seem petty. Gregory does not mention that she showed the poem to Pound, who raised no objection to her characterization of their quarrel. As the title suggests, Lowell focused on Pound's imperfect vision, his inability to take in the world as it is and make something of it. He was always off in a world of his own. "Pound has only found Pound," she concludes in *A Critical Fable*, " a poet with his own atmosphere."

C. David Heymann, *American Aristocracy: The Lives & Times of James Russell, Amy & Robert Lowell,* presents Pound even more sympathetically than most biographers do:

> Fully aware that she was a member of the wealthy and influential Lowell family of Massachusetts, Pound handled her with kid gloves. He deeply revered the class she represented. His genuflections before bloated members of that crowd, man and women with money and position, were generally well known. Then, too, Pound was milder in those days and more charming than time and politics would make him.

It is right to warn against reading into early Pound the later fascist crank, although it is difficult not to detect an incipient intolerance on his part and a wild streak. How to square Heymann's portrait with the buffoon "holding a small bathtub above his head"? Heymann does not try.

Pound's ridicule of Lowell is especially provoking because nearly all versions of the scene show her behaving with great composure. This is Richard Benvenuto's conclusion. He relies on John Gould Fletcher's memoir, *Life is My Song*, in which Lowell in repose seems a far more reliable leader than the erratic Ezra. After all, Fletcher, H. D., and Aldington, in particular, were quite young, embarking on the beginning of their careers, and ready to respond to a steady but not intrusive hand. Lowell could lead precisely because she was excited by their work but not excitable and did not pretend to be their superior. On the contrary, she treated Imagism as a truly collective enterprise.

Unlike Heymann, Fletcher is forthright about the threat Lowell posed to Pound:

> The atmosphere from the start was one of embarrassed expectancy. The fact that Amy had definitely flung down a challenge to Ezra was known to most of us. I felt the dinner might break up in some sort of quarrel . . . the hostility between him [Ford Madox Ford] and Miss Lowell was already rising to a head . . . [Ford had said the only Imagists present were H. D. and Aldington] . . . in marched Ezra, flushed and disheveled, bearing upon his head a large tin bathtub, of the old-fashioned round-edged variety, to the amazement and consternation of all present. . . . Ezra carefully deposited the unwieldy object on the floor, swept back the dank, disheveled locks from his forehead, and addressed the gathering.[5]

In Heymann, Pound is hefting a small bathtub over his head; in Fletcher, the bathtub is large and Pound appears awkward. If the tub was meant as some kind of hit at Lowell, then the larger, the better. Notice also, that Fletcher reports just how disturbing the group found Pound's entrance. Aldington, Fletcher, and H. D. were quite earnest about their new work and looking for support. Pound's antics were not a *jeu d'esprit*; they were a nasty joke. The bad taste of this occasion was intensified, moreover, by the association he made between the old-fashioned tin tub and Lowell's poem, "In a Garden," which he had accepted for the group's anthology, *Des Imagistes*. The poem echoes Walt Whitman's eroticism, especially in the last two stanzas:

> And I wished for night and you.
> I wanted to see you in the swimming-pool,
> White and shining in the silver-flecked water.
> While the moon rode over the garden,
> High in the arch of night,
> And the scent of the lilacs was heavy with stillness.
> Night, and the water, and you in your whiteness, bathing!

Did Pound's bathtub burlesque also mean something more personal? Ada Russell's presence may have lent a peculiar *frisson* to Pound's bathtub burlesque. In sum, he was attacking Lowell both personally and professionally. To perhaps save everyone embarrassment, Lowell, according to Fletcher, mildly commented that Ezra must have his joke.

Perhaps certain biographers have shied away from Fletcher's memoir because he was already writing negative letters to Lowell about Pound before the bathtub brou-ha-ha, and afterwards became Lowell's close ally. And yet his summing-up of the scene surely explains why the Imagists gravitated toward Lowell:

> Everyone felt, as I did, that we now owed homage to the gallant spirit of this woman who had brought us together, and who had maintained her position with unruffled dignity under the most difficult circumstances. . . . The evening ended in a general display of high spirits, a good deal of it at Ezra's own expense, which he was forced to bear as he best might, his face twitching at every reference to his own Wild West upbringing.

Richard Aldington, *Life for Life's Sake: A Book of Reminiscences,* corroborates Fletcher, although a pro-Poundian, I suppose, would note that Aldington was in the Lowell camp. Yet Aldington seems square, admitting he did not think much of Lowell's early poetry. Rather, she provides a way out of his bondage to Pound, whom Aldington describes as a "czar": "[H]e had the bulge on us, because it was only through him that we could get our poems into Harriet Monroe's *Poetry*, and nobody else at that time would look at them." And Aldington grew to have confidence in her judgment, especially her courting of D. H. Lawrence, a "much greater writer" than Pound.

About the bathtub scene, Aldington detected no animus on Lowell's part, concluding:

> Amy came out well that evening. There was not a trace of condescension in her and she did a difficult thing well—she expressed her warm admiration for Lawrence's work without flattery or insincerity and without embarrassing him. It is the fashion now to write off Amy as a society woman, who would never have been heard of as a writer if she hadn't been a Lowell. This is unfair. In Amy there was something of an artist and a real aesthetic appreciation. She could not have felt such enthusiasm for Lawrence and H.D. without it.

Aldington's verdict is all the more impressive because of his tactful phrasing. Note his observation that in Lowell "there was something of an artist and a real aesthetic appreciation." Thus he backs away from her with faint praise. If he does not vindicate the poet, he does redeem the person.

In the tradition of Pound biography, however, the beat goes on—as I discovered in Charles Norman's *Ezra Pound*.

He begins with the standard typecasting: "Ensconced like a queen in a suite in the Berkeley Hotel, with a view across Piccadilly to the Green Park, Amy Lowell sent the letter of introduction Harriet Monroe had given her, and Pound came to dinner." She is upset, as Norman would have it, because only "In a Garden" has been selected for *Des Imagistes*. But it is just as likely—perhaps even more so—that she was thrilled to be included in the new anthology, or even concerned that she did not have enough good work yet for a showing. Else, why pursue Pound? She understood quite well that she was just beginning to find her form.

Norman virtually destroys his credibility when he describes Lowell arguing literary principles with Ford and then returning to her hotel suite in July 1914 in a rage: "It could not have been an exchange of views; it must have been an attempt on one side or the other, or both, at violent conversion." Norman is not a very scrupulous biographer. He has Lowell puffing on a cigar while exclaiming she is an Imagist when she first reads about Imagist principles. How does he know?

Norman's version of the tub event emphasizes the talk about vorticism. He has Lowell sitting "as stiff and straight as her stoutness would permit, and clearly vexed by the performance." This is in response to Upward's making Lowell the bather in "In a Garden." How does Norman know about her posture? And he states that "everyone was doubled over with laughter, except the author." Everyone? And doubled over? The cliché makes the picture dubious.

When I checked Norman's source, John Cournos's *Autobiography*, I read that "every one at the table was shaking with laughter." This may seem a quibble, but surely it is not the biographer's province to invent details not supplied by a source recollecting a scene that occurred twenty years earlier. Cournos, an extragant admirer of Pound, claims that Lowell disliked him at first sight. He did not like her, and like many of Lowell's detractors, he invented a psychology for her: "I dare say she was in her way an unhappy woman, for she was never to know if fame would have been hers if the fates had decreed that she should struggle for recognition without the material advantages to which she was born." Cournos assumed that she was trying to buy her way into the Imagist circle. But her wealth hardly explains a career that went far beyond Cournos's limited talents and powers of perception.

Humphrey Carpenter, *A Serious Character: The Life of Ezra Pound* seems in competition with Norman to provide more details than can possibly be verified. He reports that Pound brings in a large galvanized tub and actually says to Lowell that she "might like to display her own whiteness by bathing in this vessel." It is not clear where Carpenter gets his information. The scene seems preposterous. Like Norman, he is certain of Lowell's rage at Pound's performance, which might be so if Pound was as crude as Carpenter suggests. It is more likely that Pound's actions, not his words, are the issue. Philip Callow, *Son and Lover: The Young D. H. Lawrence,* notes that Pound often made a fool of himself and provoked scenes intended to restore him to the center of attention. Thus he became fretful during one of Yeats's interminable monologues and began chewing a tulip in a dinner table vase. The more Yeats talked, the more Pound masticated flowers.

Like most of the Pound biographers, Ben F. Johnson III, *Fierce Solitude: A Life of John Gould Fletcher*, sells Lowell short: "Yet, because she knew so little of poetry and art, Fletcher could consider himself an equal, a partner, ushering her from the innocence of the old era into the authentic reality of the new." This is all wrong. Lowell knew much more about art and literature than Johnson seems to understand. By the age of 10 she had traveled with her father to Germany, visiting important museums. She was already an avid theatergoer absorbing the classics of the Western stage and writing about them in her journal. At age 14 she was already recording her reading of *Punch*, and she wrote stories and dreamed of becoming a photographer when she got her first camera in 1889. Writing poetry in her teenage years, she also enjoyed German opera and attempted to write a full-length play. By 1903 she was giving public talks about literature, citing the authorities of her age such as Hippolyte Taine and Edward Dowden, with allusions also to John Dryden, Matthew Arnold, and other earlier critics. That she was new to Imagism is hardly surprising, since the group had just been formed.

Harry T. Moore, *The Priest of Love: A Life of D. H. Lawrence* sums up the Lowell/Pound encounter: "Pound, behaving like a hedgehog trying to discourage a bear, was resisting this massive, hearty, and wealthy Bostonian who had so recently broken away from traditional poetry." Given Lowell's bulk, it is all too easy for biographers to picture Pound trying to divert her attention with a tin tub rather than try an assault head-on. But Pound was the brash, bullying party in this conflict. While Lowell certainly knew how to exert her power, she was also behaving—as he never could—as a seeker, not a prophet, an enabler, not a chieftain. Moore himself shows how she was able to attract D. H. Lawrence—not by Poundian dialectics but by the very terse, concrete, and immediate approach that distinguished Imagism. When she invited him to join her, the Aldingtons, Fletcher, and F S. Flint, he declared he was no Imagist. She responded, Moore reports, by quoting from Lawrence's poem, "Wedding Morn": "The morning breaks like a pomegranate / In a shining crack of red...." From then on, she had Lawrence's allegiance.

This brief episode suggests how an incisive Amy Lowell cut through the Poundian blather, demonstrating, as well, that she had the interests of her fellow poets in mind rather than Pound's dictates about great poetry. While he fulminated against reducing poetry to some sort of democratic denominator, she concerned herself with developing talent, presuming the greatness would arrive for some of then in due course—or not. The point was to make a beginning and to find an audience for their verse. This is why Aldington wrote her on December 26, 1914: "We are deeply grateful to you for the trouble & expense you have been to over the anthology. . . . the remaining band of us, loyal, open & disinterested, as I believe we are, should not only make a stir in the world but, what is more important, produce work of first-rate quality." When I read Aldington's letters in Lowell's collection at the Houghton Library, Harvard University, they seemed like the unaffected, sincere letters of a young man unafraid to criticize weaknesses in her poems precisely because she had been so open with him.

In *The Thorn of a Rose: Amy Lowell Reconsidered*, Glenn Richard Ruihley's commentary on Amy Lowell's reputation helps explain why so many Pound biographers have looked at Lowell awry: "A spirit as free and generous as that of Miss Lowell (and a poetic performance so halting) could never satisfy the narrow, dogmatic, and reactionary conceptions of these two men [Eliot and Pound]." That Lowell knew as much is evident in the way she groups these two together in *A Critical Fable*. Lowell's lines are not fair to either poet, but they do reveal why they rejected her. She was demotic and vulgar and keen to enlarge the audience for poetry, whereas

> Each man feels himself so little complete,
> That he dreads the least commerce with the man in the street.
> Each imagines the world to be leagued in a dim pact
> To destroy his immaculate taste by its impact.

Lowell at her best was open to showing the world's impact on her, and she despised the way Eliot and Pound sat in judgment. She had striven hard to be more than a Lowell and to reach out to a larger world. Eliot and Pound, on the other hand, "seldom bother their wits/ With outsiders at all."

It is ironic that Lowell's poetry—aimed at an audience far broader than Eliot and Pound could hope for—has suffered neglect while theirs has prospered. Ruihley claims that as the "followers of Eliot and Pound, the so-called 'new critics,' gained decisive control over literary opinion beginning in the 1930s., Miss Lowell was first ignored and then universally denigrated." Certainly Pound's high standing has colored reactions to his encounters with Lowell. As Ruilhey concludes, "The story of Miss Lowell's break with Pound, her teacher, has been recounted many times but the facts are usually slanted in Pound's favor."

Richard Benvenuto questions whether Lowell's declining reputation can really be the result of the new critics' hegemony, and certainly other explanations come to mind, including Ruihley's own admission that Lowell's poetry was "halting"— that is, it stumbled and faltered and seemed only occasionally to approach greatness. So it has been hard to find a shape to her body of work, or to filter out her very best poems.[6] In turn, this failure to process the best Lowell means that the figure of Amy Lowell is presented as unfit for the company of Eliot, Pound, et. al. Not only her accomplishments but also her motivations are suspect.

Ruihley's rehabilitation of Lowell succeeds only fitfully because his rhetoric tends toward the abstract and focuses more on her intentions than on her achievements. But his grasp of what Imagism meant to her is one of the best explanations of what Pound meant to Lowell and why she remained ever grateful to him.

Ruihley begins by describing Pound's note on the image in *Poetry* (1913). The Imagist poem places us "beyond time and space," offering a "sense of sudden growth." experienced in the presence of great art. . . . So the element at the heart of the new poetry is in the nature of an epiphany, which may be grasped directly through insight but cannot be explained by reason." Many commentators have troubled over Lowell's exclamation after reading Pound on Imagism. How could she cry out that she was an Imagist when she had not yet written any Imagist poetry? Their befuddlement serves only to exaggerate Lowell's seeming ignorance, the striving of the clubwoman (to use Horace Gregory's demeaning term) for a greatness she cannot comprehend. But Lowell was not applying a verdict to her accomplishments, or even declaring she understood Imagism. On the contrary, she was having an epiphany, an insight into the poet she wanted to become. She was, in other words, identifying with her future, saying I am what I am about to become. To have declared something less—such as "I want to be an Imagist" or "I feel like I could be an Imagist"--would indeed have shown her to be a kind of pretender. What thrilled her was the notion of "sudden growth" --the very leap in achievement she would exhibit in her second volume, *Sword Blades and Poppy Seed*.

To Lowell, the Eliot/Pound world of poetry was hermetic. As Ruihley observes, the

> practical effect of Amy Lowell's actions was to convert Imagism from a brief episode in Pound's erratic career to a powerful movement which helped to reshape American poetry. Acting alone or with his reticent followers, Pound was incapable of the effort required to overcome the inertia and conservatism of American poetry. Frozen in its insipid and moralizing Victorian forms... an incipient insurrection in the arts had found a great leader.... Without her, the major figures may have performed in much the same way—but to an empty hall in a country too occupied with "business as usual" to pay serious heed to some of the most individual and exacting poets who have ever written. The great national venture of the "new poetry" from

1914 to 1925 may be said to have been Amy Lowell's part in the evolution of our artistic life.

It is this public that Eliot and Pound turned away from, Lowell implied, when she emphasized their roles as expatriates. Unlike them, she was not afraid to make poetry a national cause, a way to enrich public life, and the country's sense of itself. No doubt she oversold the "new poetry" and herself. As she said of herself in *A Critical Fable*:

> When I push at a wheel it must go or I'll break it,
> Once embarked on a mission I never forsake it.

There is such a thing as trying too hard. Amy Lowell was a victim of a success that could not be sustained because it depended on an assembly line of products. Even supporters like Louis Untermeyer, who produced the edition of her complete poems, could not bring themselves to sort through her *oeuvre*. In part, I think the figure of Lowell herself stood in Untermeyer's way. And it is not likely that her true measure will be taken until both her life and her writing are measured together in a narrative that relies far less on the fixed notions of those all too ready to see a figure ingrained in other biographies like a palimpsest, so that each "new" biography writes over the words of the old.

P.S. After completing a draft of this chapter, I obtained a copy of Hugh Kenner's influential, if disputable, *The Pound Era*. His view of Lowell is certainly the most snide and condescending treatment of her this side of Clement Wood's scurrilous attack. Here's how he begins:

> Meanwhile, in a crystal cloud above Brookline, Mass., far darting Apollo was preparing to smite with an illumination Amy Lowell, the "hippopoetess," to

argue with whom, Carl Sandburg once remarked, was "like arguing with a big blue wave."

Kenner portrays the Lowells as loonies, likening Amy's discovery of her vocation as poet (her "illumination") with her brother Percival's claim to have discovered canals on Mars. Like her brother who founded an observatory to "follow the matter up," Amy established her own organization of poets to foster her career. Kenner's choice of archaic language (she "hied herself twice from Massachusetts to the Imagist headquarters in London") makes of her a sort of relic of a bygone age.

Kenner quotes some of Lowell's intemperate remarks about Pound—hardly worse than what many others in Pound's circle said about him—and implies that her arrogance is of a piece with her ignorance, especially in regard to her criticisms of Pound's translations of Chinese poetry, a field she claimed for herself on the basis of her brother Percival's travels in Asia and the art he brought home with him which she had been absorbing since childhood. Lowell was far too confident of her ability to master Chinese poetry, to be sure, and her dismissals of Pound's translations were too facile. No one would bank their interest in Lowell on the basis of her translations, so why is Kenner at such pains to disparage her? His assault has the effect of taking the focus off of Pound, so that Kenner feels no need to inquire why it was that the preposterous figure he enjoys exposing could possibly command the attention, let alone the respect, of H. D., Richard Aldington, and D. H. Lawrence.

But Kenner's animus toward Lowell is mild compared to Ford Madox Ford's in a piece that arrived from interlibrary loan after I had completed the foregoing analysis. In a tribute to the sculptor Gaudier-Brzeska who died in World War I fighting for France, Ford delivered in the *English Review* a broadside against "a monstrously obese Neutral whom I much disliked."⁷

Lowell's name is never used and no one else is named either except for the sculptor whose "grace of person and of physique"—ancient Greek-like in Ford's reminiscence—supplies the ideal against which the "monstrously fat, monstrously moneyed" Lowell is scorned. That Ford should have been so repulsed by Lowell's figure is curious since Rebecca West compared him to a pink whale but without "cetacean firmness." In fact, she thought he resembled a dying pig "a minute after the beginning of his collapse. He had a mouth full of crowded, misplaced teeth, and adenoids that made it difficult for him to breathe. Out of his perpetually open mouth his voice issued with strange sound effects. West remembered him talking to the artist Wyndham Lewis about the decoration of a mantelpiece: "I find it, whoof, so restful, honk." He had prominent blue eyes and hair that was like chicken down. He moved very slowly, "as if his limbs and torso were so many sacks of chaff held together by a flimsy covering."⁸

Foster Damon dutifully acknowledged Ford's account in a footnote, but evidently could not bear to deal with it—or perhaps thought it so off the mark that it was not worth rebutting. Even to refute Ford would mean quoting him and that would entail conjuring disgusting images of Lowell that her biographer, I suspect, was keen to avoid—especially since Ada Russell was sure to request that Damon delete Ford's portrayal of Lowell as leaning "monstrously sideways, devouring—devouring at once with gluttony and nonchalance."⁹ Even the most negative attacks on Lowell rarely used the word obese, favoring the less pejorative "stout" instead. But Ford loathed the dinner, calling it "The Story of a Low Tea-Shop," in which those gathered for a "disagreeable occasion—evil passions, evil people, bad, flashy cooking in an underground haunt of pre-14 smartness."

Why then was Ford there? Regarded as the "Grandfather of the Vorticists," he apparently decided his presence was therefore required. He does not say so, but he implies he attended only out of this sense of obligation. But to whom? The more one reads Ford's account, the less sense it makes. The "evil people," after all, were his friends. Yet he says he "was ordered to be there." Ford was by far the most important literary figure at the table, so who could possibly have done the ordering is rather a mystery. But he takes us into his confidence by letting slip, "You know, the dinner was a parade," one of those affairs in which the honored guest (Lowell) was to be impressed with speeches "directed at the Neutral's breeches pockets."

The food was bad as only food can be when receiving "hospitality from a person whom I dislike," Ford wrote. In blind hatred Ford turns Lowell into an object:

> It talked about its motor-car, which apparently was at Liverpool or Southampton—somewhere where there were liners, quays, cordage, cranes—all ready to abandon a city which would be doomed should Armageddon become Armageddon. The speeches went on . . .

Why Lowell should not have been made nervous about the impending war and about her possessions is only implied by the contrast with Gaudier-Brzeska who returned to France from London when he manifestly could have sat out the war like other writers Ford ridicules for finding "excuses that should keep them from the trenches." Gaudier-Brzeska, "the greatest genius of them all," never hesitated to do his part in the war because he was a man, Ford emphasizes, that was his own man, seeking neither favor nor fortune.

How then to account for the sculptor's presence at this collocation of sycophants?

> [I]t was amazing to see him there since he seemed so entirely inspired by inward visions that one wondered what he could be after—certainly not the bad dinner, the attentions of the foreign waiters, a tug at the Neutral's money-bag strings. No, he spoke as if his eyes were fixed on a point within himself; and yet with such humour and such good humour—as if he found the whole thing so comic!

This ideal artist is, of course, a projection of Ford Madox Ford. Like Gaudier-Brzeska, Ford saw himself as above the fray, although he exhibits none of Gaudier-Brzeska's good humor. Ford, a writer often twitted for his constitutional inability to tell the truth, to record a scene with anything like fidelity to what actually happened, turned the dinner with Lowell into a literary conceit.

Ford makes no mention of the bathtub incident since he is not concerned with recording what actually happened at the meal. Besides, commenting on Pound's antics would have undercut Ford's portrayal of the grotesque Lowell. A far more established figure than Pound, Ford had nothing to fear from Lowell's London expedition, and yet he obviously resented her as an interloper and, even worse, a craven imposter.

That Ford's Lowell is largely a figment of his imagination is apparent in the testimony of Pound himself. He did not deny her a certain charm; indeed what troubled him about her is that she had so successfully commandeered not merely the loyalty but the affection of the Imagists. As he wrote to Margaret Anderson, editor of *The Little Review*:

> Is there any life into which the personal Amy would not bring rays of sunshine? Is there anyone who would not delight in Amy's companionship? Alas! and alas, only, that the price i.e. equal sufferage [sic] in a

> republic of poesy; a recognition of artistic equality, should come between us.[10]

For all her feudal ways, it was the engaging demotic Lowell that Pound loathed.

Yet Ford had a point, neatly summed up in biographer Alan Judd's sentence. Reporting Ford's complaint that he really had no idea what Imagism was and he suspected that was true of the entire company present at that dinner, Judd concludes that "intellectual pretension was never one of his [Ford's] vices." Imagism, Vorticism—none of these terms could possibly describe the variety of writing these poets produced. Such terms were merely conveniences—goads—that Lowell & Co. employed to demolish the stodgy mannerisms of contemporary poets and to make a name for newcomers.

The truth is that no account of the July 17, 1914 dinner is entirely satisfactory. I read with amazement, for example, Claire Healey's report that the wives of Ford and Pound attended the dinner.[11] Did they say anything? Did anyone record their reactions? Damon, at least, had Ada Russell's memories to draw on, although he never refers directly to her recollections.

Lowell herself seemed greatly amused by the dinner and by Ford's antics, writing on September 17, 1914 to Richard Aldington that earlier that month Ford had told her he was, after all, the "only real Imagist and all its doctrines were derived from him!!!" On June 23, 1915, she wrote Aldington again to tell him she realized that Ford had taken an immediate dislike to her, and she had formed the opinion that he was an "unreliable person."[12] But his hostility did not ruffle her. "It won't make any difference," she assured Aldington, "we have gone beyond needing his help."

Claire Healey believes that Lowell's poem, "The Dinner Party," aptly describes the July 1917 dinner:

> So . . . they said,
> With their wine glasses delicately poised
> Mocking at the thing they cannot understand
> So . . . they said again
> Amused and insolent.
> The silver on the table glittered,
> And the red wine in the glasses
> Seemed the blood I had wasted
> In a foolish cause.

Was this Lowell's reaction in her heart of hearts? One reading of the poem makes her involvement in the Imagist cause a matter of regret. She watched these sophisticates divert themselves at her expense. She was not deserving of their respect, although, in truth, they were incapable of appreciating her cause. Their very disdain, however, made her feel that she had given her all to a silly project and made a sacrifice of herself for nothing.

But Lowell published this poem in 1916, when she was still very much involved with the Imagists and working indefatigably on their behalf, making sure they received their royalties from the anthologies she supervised into production. And quite another interpretation of the poem is possible, even preferable: The point of view conveys the speaker's imagining how "they" concluded that she had expended herself in a "foolish cause." The wine that metamorphoses into her blood represents her life force they are feeding on. These smug superior diners continue to talk, unaware of their own inhumanity and stupidity. In this reading, the poem is more than a covert comment on that dinner in July 1914. Lowell treats this posh meal, as revealing a carnal ferocity in this civilized group that their exquisite composure belies.

3

"A Sort of Congenital Understanding": Amy Lowell and D. H. Lawrence

Of all the figures associated with Lowell in the Imagist movement, D. H. Lawrence is the most intriguing because, as he said, he was no Imagist—although Imagist-like poems are certainly part of his oeuvre. Lawrence did not seem to think much of the Imagists. He hated their "glib irreverence about the war." To Harriet Monroe, he wrote, "How dare Amy talk about bohemian glass and stalks of flame?" Married to a German woman and having to put up with suspicions about his loyalty to Great Britain, Lawrence confessed, "it breaks my heart, this war."[13] And as to Imagism itself, he later told Witter Byner, "it was all nonsense."

But Lowell coaxed him into the movement for a while. He bowed to what he called her "ambitious insistence." And so he appeared in her Imagist anthologies. "His attitude was apparently amused consent"—or so Byner interpreted Lawrence's shrug and "cat smile."[14] This would not be the last time that Lawrence would affect a studied aloofness on the subject of Amy Lowell.

For her part, Lowell never doubted Lawrence's genius, and the plight of the man disturbed her. In World War I London, she visited him and later told Byner of her dismay at Lawrence's "deplorably dingy, airless basement, harmful not only to his spirit but to his health." Perhaps because of her work on John Keats, she was immediately attuned to his tubercular condition, which seemed to have accentuated his keyed-up, nervous nature. The irritable Lawrence seemed to her "opinionated and willful," but that did not deter her from championing his cause. Indeed, she commanded Byner to do what he could for the Lawrences.[15]

Lowell and Lawrence enjoyed a significant exchange of letters—in itself proof that the bond between them was far deeper than Lawrence wanted to acknowledge to others. What did they see in each other, and how have their biographers presented the Lowell and Lawrence duo—a seemingly unlikely convergence of two very different writers and personalities? As usual, I am keenly interested in how biographers describe and develop Lowell as a character in their narratives. When I began research for this chapter, I wondered whether the Lawrence biographers would finally do justice to Lowell—or at least improve on the poor performance of most Pound and Frost biographers. Much more than in previous chapters, I will have primary sources to rely on—chiefly letters—and not just memoirs and second-hand accounts. As a result, I will be seeking to define the understanding that Lowell and Lawrence had between them and measure that against what the biographers say. This sandwich structure will reveal, I hope, the tensions between autobiography and biography.

In *D. H. Lawrence: The Man and His Work*, Emile Delevenay describes his subject as a "socially maladjusted man." Certainly Lawrence, the restless traveler, never seemed to find his place. He changed addresses so often that Amy Lowell found it difficult to keep track of his whereabouts. Books she sent him went astray, although the ever-practical Amy never sent him money unless she was sure it would arrive before the next move. As if to compensate for a peripatetic existence that threatened to interrupt his lines of communication, Lawrence was a faithful correspondent who gave more of himself in his letters to Lowell than she was able to reciprocate—for reasons no biographer seems ever to have investigated. Lawrence surely detected her reticence, although he never commented on it in their epistolary exchanges. Why did he keep writing to her? He wrote more letters to her than she could bring herself to answer—as she herself regretted in one of her notes to him. Although Lawrence did occasionally berate her to others—as certain biographers report—he discovered a rapport between himself and Lowell that he described as "a sort of congenital understanding." Why he used that particular phrase has not been explored—perhaps because most of those writing on this pair have viewed her as not much more than Lawrence's sounding board and bankable supporter. Yet he was too magnificent of a human being and a writer to waste his words on a mere source of sympathy and ready cash. He took a greater level of interest in Lowell than was strictly necessary for one seeking her largesse. She made it clear that her belief in his literary greatness was unshakable, and that it gave her pleasure to praise him and to promote his work no matter what he thought of hers. He did not have to try hard to please her or indulge in flattery. He never thought of her as a great poet—perhaps not even a good one—as she seemed to recognize. And yet she had something it was worth his while to seek. What it was is a matter of conjecture and surmise, the probing of an affinity that neither one ever explicitly acknowledged. The point to grasp, though, is that their relationship held for a decade—even though it was based on only one fortunate meeting—ceasing only when she died. And the longevity of their correspondence is even more remarkable because, as

Delevenay points out, Lawrence engaged in a "ceaseless quest for friendship, often doomed to cruel disappointment."

The unsentimental Jeffrey Meyers sees little to explain in the Lowell/Lawrence affiliation:

> Lawrence's friendship with Lowell, unlike his others, was based on mutual exploitation. The extreme individualist benefited from the money and influence of his only personal contact in America, while the crude careerist captured his poetic genius for her Amygistic anthologies. She tried to collect royalties owed to Lawrence by the slippery American publisher Mitchell Kennerley, and at Frieda's request sent money during and after the war to the sick and penniless Lawrence, who, in March 1921, described the sinking lady as "trying to keep afloat on the gas of her own importance: hard work, considering her bulk."

Meyers provides no context for Lawrence's cruel dismissal of Lowell as a gasbag and can imagine her as exciting only Lawrence's rarely expressed mercenary side. As a "crude careerist" she is hardly worth the biographer's attention, especially since Lawrence serves exclusively as an Amygistic enterprise. Meyers also conveys the impression that Lowell sent Lawrence money only at the request of the latter's wife—not an accurate or fair idea of the role money played in their relationship.[16] Finally, what are we to make of the "sinking lady" phrase that plays off of wording in a Lawrence letter? Are we to presume that Lowell's reputation is sinking in Lawrence's estimation? But he never had a high opinion of her work to begin with, and at the time Lowell was enjoying some of her best reviews and tributes as a leading voice in contemporary poetry. More likely, it seems, Meyers is referring obscurely to Lowell's failing health, occasioned by a hernia that proved irreparable and that would be the proximate cause of her stroke and sudden death in May 1925.

Describing Lawrence's rather trying period of residence in New York City, Meyers notes that the Lawrences were supposed to visit the

> generous but irritating Amy Lowell in Boston. But they were now too distracted and angry to do so. Lawrence's uneasy *de haut en bas* relations with Amy surfaced when he wrote: "Not having a secretary to [type and] sign my letter I sign it myself," and when he gave his Sicilian landlord, coming to work in Boston, a letter of introduction, Amy, who could not conceive of a connection with a cook, replied: "I will look up your Sicilian, although I cannot see what good it will do as I am not by way of being able to employ him." Amy had, at first, defended her literary territory and discouraged Lawrence's visit to America and to Boston. Then she relented, and invited him for three days. But Lawrence, using the excuse of Frieda's urgent dental appointment in New York, decided not to go.

That Lawrence resented having to rely on Lowell for hospitality and funds he freely admitted to Lowell herself in more than one letter. But he expected her to understand his annoyance— as much with himself as with her—and she did. And why she dreaded his trip to America in spite of earlier encouragement is a much more complicated matter than the brisk Meyers is willing to consider.

In *Lawrence and the Women*, Elaine Feinstein begins with the first and only meeting between Lowell and Lawrence-- where any full accounting of what they meant to each other must begin and ultimately end. At dinner with the Aldingtons in July 1914, Lowell places Lawrence "at her side as the guest of honour, expressing her admiration for his work." Lawrence "enjoyed the warmth of Lowell's praise. Amy Lowell may have been obese and bossy, but she had a genuine and discriminating love of poetry, and was a loyal champion of Lawrence and H. D., among others." As if an obese person cannot be discriminating in her love of poetry? An unfortunate choice of words that reflects an inherent bias against Lowell in most accounts where her wealth and weight count against her, if only by implication. Feinstein's bias is milder than Meyers's, but her *image* of Lowell prevents the biographer from a full appreciation of the scene. Even so, Feinstein treats Lawrence's response to Lowell much more generously—that is, without Meyers's cynicism. After explaining how Lowell worked to publish Lawrence and get him paid for his work as well as sending him money, Feinstein concludes, "Lawrence in turn was solicitous about her health, wrote sympathetically when she was grieving for her brother, and was moved by her generosity even when it was elicited by a begging letter from Frieda." Meyers doubts that Lowell could genuinely move Lawrence because, I suspect, Meyers is constitutionally incapable of regarding Lowell favorably. I draw this conclusion not only from what he has written about Lowell but also from conversations and correspondence we have had about her. His descriptions of Lowell and Lawrence posit an either/or world: either the two poets are using one another or the inconceivable alternative: they actually liked and empathized with one another. But both alternatives could be true—which is the subtext of Feinstein's view of the two. She also introduces another aspect of the Lowell/Lawrence nexus when she notes that Lawrence was not "obsequious, and could deliver a sudden rebuke," but I will deal with that aspect of their relationship when I discuss their letters.

In *The Priest of Love*, Harry T. Moore portrays the first and only meeting between Lowell and Lawrence with undue tentativeness: "Lawrence evidently enjoyed the talk that went back and forth across the table in Amy Lowell's suite on that evening of July 30, 1914. The next day he wrote to Harriet Monroe that he had dined with Amy Lowell and the Aldingtons, 'and we had some poetry'." During their decade of correspondence Lawrence would mention on several occasions how much he enjoyed that first meeting, and Lowell certainly felt the same. It was fun to be in her witty company—a fact often forgotten in references to her as bossy and imperious. Not then—in July 1914—or at any point in her letters to him does this highhanded side of Lowell appear. On the contrary, she treats him as nothing less than a great man, and it is hard to see how her expressions of support are part of a "crude careerism." What, in 1921, for example, could Lawrence have done for Lowell? She had far more influence than he did and often better reviews as well. He needed her much more than she needed him, yet her encouraging tone never wavered—not even when he criticized her work.

Indeed Lowell treated Lawrence with the utmost sensitivity. At the beginning, she sent him no checks but rather tried to extract royalties on Lawrence's behalf from his American publishers. Lawrence's biographers note this fact but do not seem to understand its purport. Lowell was not dispensing charity from on high. She was helping a fellow poet and even doing his grunt work. Before she knew Lawrence well, she also sent him a typewriter, telling Harriet Monroe that this might be the most tactful way to help him out. Indeed he was quite grateful—even exhilarated by her thoughtful gift. Lowell also urged Monroe to send Lawrence payment for his poems that Monroe should publish sooner rather than later. Only when Frieda wrote asking Lowell directly for money, did Lowell feel it appropriate to send it. But I'm getting ahead of the story—poor as it is—that the Lawrence biographers tell.

In the early stages of her friendship with Lawrence, Lowell was careful to do the practical considerate things that a fellow writer would appreciate. She obviously did not want him to think of her as his patron. She was fond of saying God made her a businesswoman but she made herself a poet. She was also careful not to confuse these two different aspects of herself when dealing with Lawrence. That she knew how to conduct business was a boon to her fellow Imagist poets. She kept track of their royalties and made sure they were paid promptly. What professional writer has not complained about publishers delaying payment? It is *the cause of great concern*—all those hours spent working, the press of deadlines, and then the dreadful wait for the check. To do anything that would ameliorate this infuriating, frustrating process of earning a living from writing could only be welcomed with intense gratitude.

Moore supposes that Lowell panicked when she learned of Lawrence's intentions to visit the United States. Like other Lawrence biographers, Moore does not seem to wonder why she was "terrified" at the prospect of Lawrence visiting New England. Meyers supposes that Lowell for some reason feared competition from Lawrence, whereas Moore (relying on a fairly narrow reading of Lowell's letters to Lawrence) repeats her view that puritanical Boston would reject Lawrence who already had quite a reputation for his erotic work. She also feared, with some reason, that Lawrence (although he denied it) had built her country up into a sort of Eldorado. Lawrence would turn away from America, she feared, repulsed because it couldn't "see the difference between envisioning life whole and complete, physical as well as spiritual, and pure obscenities like those perpetrated by James Joyce." Her comments on Joyce might make readers question her judgment, but more is behind her assessment of Lawrence's handling of sex and love that relates to her own circumstances as much as to Lawrence's—as I will suggest in due course.

Not surprisingly, Lowell's authorized biographer, S. Foster Damon, presents the context of the Lowell/Lawrence decade in terms reflecting a deeper—although by no means complete—understanding. Lowell had not even heard of Joyce before she met Lawrence, Damon reports, whereas she already knew and admired Lawrence's writing. Then Lowell's attraction to Freida strengthened her attachment to Lawrence: "she [Lowell] was not quite sure what to expect as regards his wife. She was overwhelmed with astonishment and pleasure, however, to meet a lady of exquisite, vital presence." The rapport with this couple is reminiscent of her affection for Robert and Elinor Frost. Lowell's detractors ought really to pause at this evidence of her empathy for others rather than emphasizing that her person and her position constituted a barrier separating her from others.

Jean Gould adds little to Damon's authoritative account, except for two striking observations: Lowell loved Lawrence's dramatic entrance during her London stay announcing that the English were about to enter the war. With her own flair for the dramatic, she was drawn to a man with style. She also seems to have been taken with what Gould calls his "scrubbed appearance," so austere and quite an antidote to that sartorial showoff Ezra Pound. Gould has an engaging way of placing us in the same room with Lowell and Lawrence so that we can imagine how they charmed one another. When Lowell adopted a somewhat formal pose in her letters to Lawrence, he penetrated the veil, expressing, Gould reminds us, his appreciation for her personal poems that expressed her deep emotions and private life.

By far the best account of Lowell and Lawrence appears (to my surprise) in the usually negative Horace Gregory. His magnificent reading of their correspondence stimulated me to see in their exchanges a very moving affair that no other biographer has come close to capturing. Gregory shows that Lawrence elicited from Lowell qualities that others like Pound never knew existed. For quite different reasons, both Lowell and Lawrence stood out from the literary society they inhabited but were never quite comfortable with. As Gregory puts it, Lawrence described himself as a writer

> apart from groups and movements, a position that brought respect from Amy Lowell's reservoir of common sense. His appearance, despite his red hair, was in great contrast to Ezra Pound's ["slender . . . with a quick, lithe, nervous step and very blue eyes"]; his manner had the brightness, the eagerness in talk of one who had taught (which he did for three years in a boys' prep school in Croydon). He was distinctly apart form the neo-Bohemianism of the John Middleton Murry-Katherine Mansfield household . . . and of Pound. . . His appearance, which reflected his personality, held a fascination for Amy Lowell. However lightly or—in another mood—perceptively he talked, he took time out for listening with his vivid, blue eyes fixed on the speaker's face—as though his listening could be taken as an unspoken and direct compliment to his hostess. It is easy to understand why Amy Lowell liked him.

Like Damon, Gregory sees Frieda playing a key role: "She [Lowell] respected Frieda's calm air of being the daughter of a 'Baron' and she caught a gleam of Lawrence's intelligence." As much as Lowell liked Richard Aldington and H. D., that young couple, especially Aldington, never exhibited the kind of ease Lawrence evinced when he met Lowell. Unlike Pound, he was not trying to fit Lowell into a program, and though she courted Lawrence for her Imagist group, she never claimed too much for his work as an Imagist. In effect, his inclusion in the Imagist anthologies was a matter of convenience—chiefly for him so that he could have a forum for his poetry. Both understood this quite well without it having to be said. Lawrence saw no reason to ruffle Lowell's sensibilities given how much they had in common. So he was careful with her—or as Gregory phrases it: "Though she thought Lawrence's writings were inspired by 'some sort of erotic mania,' his tactful letters to her smoothed away any doubts she had concerning the propriety of his theories." But Lawrence's eroticism troubled her for other reasons having to do, I think, with how she expressed her own sexuality—a topic Gregory never entertains.

In a wonderful feat of empathetic imagination Gregory shows how for all their differences in background Lowell and Lawrence shared a fundamental understanding because of the worlds they had come from:

> But there were other reasons why Lawrence met Amy Lowell with deeper insight than his American contemporary Ezra Pound. In Nottingham, miner's son though he was, he had known women of Amy Lowell's kind,--her kind, that is, in respect to managing an estate the size of Sevenels. Women of the smaller gentry in Nottingham did not pretend to knowing or writing poetry, nor were they anywhere near so wealthy as Amy Lowell of Brookline, but they shared something of her common sense, her ease and tough-mindedness in business matters, and her kindliness to and sense of responsibility toward animals on her estate. In this perception, Lawrence had an advantage over other younger poets who accepted Amy Lowell's invitations to dinner. . . .

Gregory establishes how it is that after only one meeting Lawrence and Lowell should form such a sure-footed attachment to each other with none of the awkward, wary behavior that shackled his contemporaries' responses to her.

Gregory is keenly attuned to the tonal shifts of Lawrence's letters and their impact on Lowell: Lawrence's "utterly desperate, wistful letters . . . opened an unguarded chamber between her 'common sense' and her practical desire 'to do good.'" What would serve Lawrence best? is the implicit question haunting Lowell's letters to him. And Lawrence seems to have divined her need to help him as a way of salving her own sense of isolation and desperation, Gregory suggests:

> Perhaps he had guessed her love of being "on the inside of things" her hidden loneliness, her feeling of being "left out" among writers of the younger generation as well as the old. In his letters Lawrence never failed to give her something of himself, which was the kind of compliment that Amy Lowell seldom received and which he performed with instinctive artfulness.

This "something of himself" often consisted—as I will show presently—placing Lowell beside himself in the landscapes and settings of his sojourns. Although she traveled widely on lecture tours, Lowell remained primarily in Lawrence's imagination fixed in Brookline, encased in her own garden, the one place she would describe in her letters. Her garden steadied her and became her frame of reference when dealing with Lawrence's restlessness.

Lawrence felt comforted in knowing that Lowell would take his confidences to her heart and help him. He was not importunate. He wrote of his worries and aspirations as to a confidant—not a role that other writers found it possible to adopt with Amy Lowell. "Among those of the younger generation who wrote to her," Gregory notes:

> Lawrence was the only one who took the trouble to let her know that he understood her and valued the friendship between them. In his letters he exercised one of his greatest gifts—the gift of making each letter a fragment of autobiography and, in a Lawrencian sense, a work of art. He appealed to her ego rather than her vanity; to her feminine, semi-maternal instincts rather than to the fact that she was a rich woman. . . . He presented himself as an investment in greatness and a guarantee of an immortality for the investor. By these means he placed himself far above Amy Lowell's usual flatterers; he could well afford not to praise her writings indiscriminately.

Indeed, the test of his greatness was his reluctance to accord her more praise than she deserved.

No other person other than Ada Russell could speak to Lowell's deepest need—which was not to be praised per se but to be acknowledged for her self. Gregory's brilliant perceptions stop short, however, of understanding the extent to which Lowell actually did transcend her inhibitions. Because he never turns his attention to Russell and to the poems inspired by her, Gregory consigns Lowell to the emotionally deprived state that Meyers insists on. Thus Gregory writes that Lawrence appealed to "her need of being understood . . . part of her unfulfilled desire, which is so frequently expressed in the actions of a 'spoiled' child, the desire to love and be loved."

Lowell latched onto Lawrence because he "gave her a deeper reading of herself than she cared to make public . . . . It was rewarding for her to read in his comments deeper resources of her emotions than she was able to show," Gregory concludes. Thus he claims that if Lowell had only taken Lawrence's admonition to be herself she would have been a better poet. Instead she took refuge in shocking audiences, and storming their sensibilities with "vigorous Lowellese and dramatic gestures." True enough, except that Gregory ignores her lyric poems that do in fact reveal the poet herself.

The Lowell/Lawrence letters are like a conversation that is never quite concluded and remains on the cusp of revelation. Even at their most business-like these two poets reflected their personalities and postures vis a vis each other. For example, on 18 September 1914, early on in their correspondence, Lawrence asks her: "You won't forget to go to Mitchell Kennerley for me, will you? My agent writes me that he also fails utterly to arose any echo of response from the gentleman in New York." Lawrence even provides Lowell with a short script of questions to ask the wayward publisher. He could hardly have made such a request save for her firm declarations that she wanted to be of service to him. But then he bows to her, "And I kiss you hand, dear Miss Lowell, for being so good to me."

Gallant and wistful (to borrow Gregory's word), Lawrence laments his plight with a charming lilt that skirts self-pity:

> We are likely to stay in this cottage [in Buckinghamshire] till I am a silvery haired old gentleman going round patting the polls of the cottage toddlers. Nobody will pay me any money, and nobody is good to me, and already the robins are brightening to sing, and the holly berries on the hedges are getting redder. Ahimé – ahimé! ["Oh dear – Oh dear!"] It's winter, and the wooden gate is black and sodden in the rain, above the raw cold puddles. Ahimé once more. Im dunklen Laub die gold Orangen gluhn.

Did Lawrence send Lowell to her encyclopedias and dictionaries to find that he was quoting Goethe's *Wilhelm Meister*: "The golden oranges glow in the darkening foliage." This enchanting Imagist paragraph—would Lowell have regarded it as her kind of polyphonic prose?—reminded her, without having to say so, of what she and Lawrence shared. As self-absorbed as he could seem, Lawrence nevertheless went out of his way to share his world with Lowell because they agreed on certain modernist aesthetic principles. Richard Benvenuto, in his admirable introduction to Lowell, explains:

> Though reacting against the excessive subjectivity . . . of the late Victorian period, the new poets are still free to write about themselves, as well as about others and nature; but they do not emphasize or insist on the importance of the self. Lowell's position on this is very close to Lawrence's—all things are radiating "out from me," but exist independently in a "vast whole" of which the self is but a small part."

Hence Lawrence's *cri de coeur* occurs in a red-berried and robin-singing world rather like William's Carlos Williams's wheelbarrow poem but in more somber colors emanating from that slick black wooden gate and puddled cold that shivers Lawrence's soul.

This particular letter ends with the formulaic "Give our very warm regards to your friend [Ada Russell]," which becomes a refrain in his correspondence acknowledging the most important person in Lowell's life. Lawrence hardly ever wrote without some reference to Ada or to his wife Frieda. In every sense of the word, he was coupled, part of a system of two equal forces that are parallel but facing in opposite directions.

Below his signature, he added: "We've made some blackberry jelly. That's my nearest approach to poetry here." Like his mention to Harriet Monroe that his meeting with Lowell produced poetry, Lawrence made of the every day an exuberant art. Not only did he report himself "tipsy" over the typewriter she sent him but also the machine itself seemed alive, "like a bubbling pot, frightfully jolly."

By his seventh letter to Lowell (18 November 1914), Lawrence was already taking her measure, deploring her efforts to emulate Continental verse:

> I like *you* in your poetry. I don't believe in affecting France. I like you when you are straight out. . . . . Why don't you always be yourself. Why go to France or anywhere else for your inspiration. If it doesn't come out of your own heart, real Amy Lowell, it is no good, however many colours it may have. I wish one saw more of your genuine strong, sound self in this book [*Sword Blades and Poppy Seed*], full of commonsense and kindness and the restrained almost bitter Puritan passion. Why do you deny the bitterness in your nature, when you write poetry? Why do you take a pose?

He liked best "A Tulip Garden," the last poem in *Sword Blades and Poppy Seed* because of its "real old English strong gusto." Tulips are arrayed as if in battle dress: "Here infantry/ Wheels out into the sunlight. / What bold grace/ Sets off their tunics, white with crimson lace!"

Lawrence's portrait of Lowell as a passionate, bitter Puritan expresses perhaps more of what he wanted to find in her than was ever actually present. He saw a side of her akin to himself, the "fierce, feverish intensity of spirit" that interested John Gould Fletcher when he described Lawrence in *Life is My Song*. Fletcher remarked on Lawrence's bitterness and his search for a "few congenial spirits."

It is hard to believe that Lawrence had no real feeling for Lowell when he writes:

> I suppose you think me damned impertinent. But I hate to see you posturing, when there is thereby a real person betrayed in you.

> Please don't be angry with what I say. Perhaps it really is impertinence.

Is Lawrence merely temporizing in an effort to appease Lowell? I doubt it. I sense real pain in his exhortation, the distress of a man who cannot abide a friend's breaking of faith with herself, especially since in the next paragraph he cannot bear to leave his disappointment alone even as he is making his manners: "At any rate, I thank you very much for your book of poems, which I like because after all they have a lot of you in them—but how much nicer, finer, bigger you are, intrinsically, than your poetry is."

Lowell did not reply immediately to Lawrence's criticism, and her subsequent letters deal more with trying to get money out of Kennerley (it proved to be a lost cause) and making the business arrangements for the Imagist anthologies that included Lawrence's work. In general, she was far more circumspect than Lawrence, admitting only that "I am awfully down and out, but this down and outne[ss] is a chronic condition of us writers pe[rhaps]."

Eventually Lowell did answer Lawrence's charge:

> I remember your wrestling with me last year was because of my French pose. You see it is not pose, it is a reality, and if you do come to New York, you will see why it is a reality. You will realize that America is more Continental than British. The immigration that has been going on for years is having an effect, and even we who are of pure Anglo-Saxon ancestry can not help being affected by it.

Lowell had a point. It was a diverse country and Lawrence was building up in his mind a picture of an America that would serve as a kind of antidote to the Britishness he was so bitter about. She did not care much for the Puritan label that others wanted to put on her character.

Lawrence evidently worried that he had gone too far in his criticism and that is why he had quite a wait to receive Lowell's next letter. Although the letter he sent expressing his concern has been lost, Lowell adverts to his anxiety in her 1 February 1916 letter:

> Your letter of January 10th [it is missing] was very welcome. Of course, we shall remain friends. What on earth could prevent it? I am a bad correspondent, I know, but as I told you in my last letter, I am a loyal friend.

She took great pleasure in his evocative descriptions—this one of the view looking down to the sea from his Cornwall cottage:

> There are sea-pinks, like little throngs of pink bees hovering on the edge of the land, over a sea that is blue and hard like a jewel. There are myriad primroses spread out so large and cool and riskily, under the shadows, and bluebells trailing under the great granite boulders, and fox-gloves rearing up to look. It is a rather wild, rocky country, of magpies and hawks and foxes. I love it.

This sense of nature in motion, the fitting of human feelings within the organization of nature, clearly had its appeal to the author of "A Tulip Garden." It does not seem too much to say that Lawrence and Lowell lived for this kind of experience. As she wrote him in her next letter, "I do not know anybody that writes about the English countryside as you do; I had rather read what you say about it than look at it, which is a high tribute." It is also her way of saying it was *him*, not his subject matter, that attracted her.

Lawrence, in turn, seemed most attracted to what might be called her poems of pure sensation, evoking, in his words, the

> primary, elemental forces, kinetic, dynamic—prismatic, tonic, the great, massive, active *inorganic* world, elemental, never softened by life, that hard universe of Matter and Force where life is not yet known, come to pass again. It is strange and wonderful. I find it only in you & H.D., in English: in your "Bath" . . . . Of course, it seems to me this is the real *cul de sac* of art.

Lawrence wrote that he liked quite a few poems in *Men, Women, and Ghosts*, which he considered a better book than *Sword Blades and Poppy Seed*. That he should single out "Bath," is not surprising since one passage in the prose poem was very Lawrencian, perhaps reminding him of his sojourn in the Cornwall cottage overlooking a jeweled sea:

> The sunshine pours in at the bath-room window
> and bores through the water in the bath-tub in lathes
> and planes of greenish-white. It cleaves the water
> into flaws like a jewel, and cracks it to bright light.

Lawrence admired this sort of sharp, geometric (cubist? inorganic?) composition. This is nature, but nature read for what Amy Lowell does to it. Such poems may have reassured him that she was worth taking trouble over as she took trouble over him. He found in at least some of her work a temperament that complemented his own.

But Lowell, he realized, went more deeply into nature, the thing itself, than he did. In his letters, he tends to emerge out of his absorption in nature with a comment on the oncoming world: "The robin comes on to the door-step now, and watches me as I write. Soon he will come indoors. Then it will be midwinter." Lowell, on the other hand, ends "Bath":

> The sky is blue and high. A crow flaps by the window, and there is a whiff of tulips and narcissus in the air.

Is this what Lawrence meant by a *cul de sac*, an art that ends without self-consciousness and cannot go on, kinetic and tonic precisely because the human factor is reduced to a whiff?

In spite of the compliments Lowell paid to Lawrence ("you have always been successful"), he did not let up on criticizing aspects of her work that seemed inauthentic:

> *Don't* do Japanese things, Amy, if you love us. I would a million times rather have a fragment of 'Aquarium' than all the Japanese poems put together. I am so disappointed with this batch you have decided to put in, it isn't you at *all*, it has nothing to do with you, and it is not real. Alas and alas, why have you done this thing?

Lawrence seems genuinely upset with her because she can do so much better. He closes his letter of 23 March 1917 without the usual expression of regards to Ada Russell and instead exhorts Lowell: "Do write from your *real* Self, Amy, don't make up things from the outside, it is so saddening."

Like "Bath," but perhaps more so, "An Aquarium" appealed to Lawrence because it embodied his notion that Lowell led her fellow American poets in registering the "physico-sensational world, apprehension of things non-human, not conceptual":

> Streaks of green and yellow iridescence,
> Silver shiftings,

> Rings veering out of rings,
> Silver -- gold –
> Grey-green opaqueness sliding down,
> With sharp white bubbles
> Shooting and dancing.
> Flinging quickly outward.
> Nosing the bubbles,
> Swallowing them,
> Fish.

Lawrence deemed "An Aquarium" an example of "non-emotional aestheticism," and he meant it as a compliment. For him, Lowell's therapeutic value derived from her pristine perceptions, her ability to render a tangible world in its own terms in so far as language and speech rhythms could do so. At their best, Lowell's lines are tightly tethered to the shape, color, and movement of creatures we name "fish." "An Aquarium" has an uncanny ability to paint fish at a level of abstraction that resists the human, mimetic impulse to reproduce an object in space. Lowell's fish become "blue brilliance cut by black bars," "an oblong pane of straw-coloured shimmer," "a smear of rose, black, silver." Hers is a submarine world of "shadows and polished surfaces" and "facets of mauve and purple,/A constant modulation of values." This last phrase is an especially brilliant touch, linking the nonhuman and human, the perceiver and the perceived—but not as in the Romantic tradition that Wordworth defined as the poet half perceiving and half creating his world. Lawrence understood that Lowell's verse was a kind of giving over of herself to the other, nonhuman world. And she was never more herself than when in this mode of allowing "a constant modulation of values" to arise out of her perceptions. Or as Lawrence put it, she was unlike the English who "still see with concepts." Lowell, in other words, did not impose herself on the world depicted in her best poems.

Lowell's response to Lawrence was curt, although it is hard to say how hurtful his verdict may have been. The Japanese poems were a perfectly authentic side of her nature, she affirmed, and not artificial. "I never in my life wrote anything that was not sincere, and personally I like these little poems as well as anything I have done." Posterity has not agreed with her, but then like many writers Lowell did not always understand the true nature of her gifts, and she certainly had a right to believe—given her long-standing interest in Japanese art—that she was not indulging in a fad. "Never in my life" sounds a little huffy, yes? But this is all Lowell had to say by way of defense.

I don't think Lowell could ever have been hard on Lawrence—not only because she admired his genius but because he had such a difficult time of it during the war, hounded by the police because of his German wife, and the subject of attacks simply because of the way he looked: "People write letters of accusation," Lawrence wrote Lowell on 13 December 1917, "because one has a beard and looks not quite the usual thing." Did Lowell think of herself while reading his words? He regarded his time with her as a kind of reprieve from a world that now did not allow him to be himself, "when we met for the first time, and laughing at ourselves. Oh my dear Amy, I do wish to heaven we could meet again in peace and freedom, to laugh together and be decent and happy with each other."

Lowell tried to cheer Lawrence by reviewing his book of poetry, *Look! We Have Come Through!*, deeming him "a man of genius." Her review is perhaps most remarkable for its attempt to put in context Lawrence's erotic art:

> He is a poet of sensation, but of sensation as the bodily efflorescence of a spiritual growth. Other poets have given us sensuous images; other poets have spoken of love as chiefly desire; but in no other poet does desire

> seem so surely the "outward and visible form of an inward and spiritual grace." Mr. Lawrence does not do this by obscuring passion in a poetical subterfuge, he gives the naked desire as it is; but so tuned is his mind that it is always the soul made visible in a supreme moment.

Lowell's language is as coded here as it is in her own erotic poems. "Supreme moment"? Is she writing of orgasm? The soul made flesh? She was as careful not to offend Lawrence's readers as she had been not to outrage her own. Indeed, so successful was she in disguising her own erotic verse that generations of critics and biographers—until the advent of Jean Gould—scarcely alluded to her sexuality, except for her harshest detractor Clement Wood, who referred to the "Sapphic fragments" of the "singer of Lesbos."

It is rather important to see that Lowell felt much the same as Lawrence about the importance of eros, although she was shocked at how far he was willing to go in employing the actual words and actions of sexual arousal in his poetry and prose. In his autobiography, John Gould Fletcher relates an episode in which Lawrence sent Lowell a poem for an Imagist anthology "so sexy in quality that she herself judged that the printers would be inclined to think it obscene." She telephoned the publisher, read the poem to him, and asked, "Now don't you think that is perfectly obscene?"

Fletcher's anecdote is second-hand, told to him by the publisher's second-in-command, so it is hard to gauge Lowell's feelings. I doubt that that she was shocked by the poem itself as much as by how it would damage Lawrence at home and abroad:

> I know there is no use in counseling you to make any concessions to public opinion in your books; and, although, I regret sincerely that you cut yourself off

by an outspokenness which the English public does not understand, I regret it not in itself . . . but simply because it keeps the world from knowing what a great novelist you are. I think that you could top them all if you would be a little more reticent on this one subject. You need not change your attitude a particle, you can simply use an India rubber in certain places, and then you can come into your own as you ought to be. But what is the use? You will turn from these remarks with a shrug of disgust and say, "Another, another. They are all against me!" Of course that is not true, and of course you must know that I do not mean it that way, but when one is surrounded by prejudice and blindness, it seems to me that the only thing to do is get over in spite of it and not constantly run afoul of these same prejudices which, after all, hurts oneself and the spreading of one's work, and does not do a thing to right the prejudice. Few people are pure minded enough as you mean them, which I tried to point out in my essay.

Amy Lowell knew her man because she knew herself so well—what it had cost her to stay within the bounds of what was then considered proper language for a poet. If it was painful to remain a closet lesbian, how much more painful it would have been to come out and suffer the kinds of rebuffs—and more—that Lawrence had endured. How keenly Lowell felt his isolation since she was also the "one" who had also had been "surrounded by prejudice and blindness." Few people would have been "pure minded" enough to accept any sort of openly avowed lesbian love lyrics. Of all Lawrence's contemporaries, Lowell could best empathize with his loneliness.

Some critics have left the impression that Lowell *was* shocked at Lawrence's outspokenness, but I take her at her word, when she writes in her letter, "I regret it not in itself." Unlike Lawrence, Lowell remained enough of a conservative not to offend society for her own sake but also for society's sake. But as a poet, she could hardly deny him his own form of expression. She was, therefore, in a bind and quite aware of why Lawrence would reject her advice. Because Lawrence had no such belief in or respect for society, no sort of compromise with himself or with others seemed feasible:

> No, Amy, again you are not right when you say the india-rubber eraser would let me through into a paradise of popularity. Without the India-rubber I am damned along with the evil, with the india-rubber I am damned among the disappointing. You see what it is to have a reputation. I give it up, and put my trust in heaven. One needn't trust a great deal in anything, & in humanity not at all.

Lawrence's response may have decided Lowell to no longer encourage him to visit America. Commentators have speculated that she did not want to take responsibility for his trip, fearing that his fragile health might result in a collapse that she would have to deal with, or that she was just not prepared to have a writer quite so powerful within her precincts. They got on so well from afar, who knows what his proximity would do to her equanimity and his prospects in the U. S. No one can say for sure what Lowell felt, although she outlined in letters to Lawrence and his wife why a visit would likely end in disaster, emphasizing, again, his controversial reputation and his tendency, she believed, to idealize America. In the end, whatever the constellation of motivations may have been, Lowell had concluded that a U.S. tour would do him no good. Even before receiving Lowell's list of objections to his trip, Lawrence sensed her attitude when he wrote on 26 May 1919: "Are you shy of me?—a little doubtful of the impression I shall, or should make? I hope not. I believe you are the only person I know, actually, in America, so I was hoping you'd help me a bit to find my feet when I come." Lawrence said he wanted to know Lowell's real feelings on the matter. Above all, his confirmation that she was the "only person" he knew in America made his visit only more risky in her view, especially when he proposed in a later letter to stay with her. It made her nervous to have guests in the house, she wrote him, especially because of her precarious health.

Lawrence did eventually visit America, and though he remained in contact with her, biographers like Jeffrey Meyers note that he found an excuse for not meeting her again. Another meeting might have been disappointing for both sides, I suppose, since both had such fond memories of their initial encounter. Perhaps even more important to them, however, was their correspondence, which had taken on a life of its own and can be viewed, really, as a separate realm—quite apart from what Lowell and Lawrence said about each other outside the bounds of their epistolary exchanges. Not only did Lawrence continue to write to Lowell, his praise for her work escalated, so that the last books of hers he was to read before her death received his highest encomium: "I read Legends last night,—and again this morning. I like them the best of all your poems. You have always written of the existence & magic of *things* . . . But in this book it is life and death superseding things. So I like this book the best.

His praise elicited from Lowell her most ebullient response. She often sent him her work saying she did not expect him to like it. She dreaded his disfavor but bore it for the sake of his greatness and resisted her impulse to argue with him. Now she opened up:

> I wonder if you have the slightest idea of how much pleasure your letter about "Legends" has given me. I know what you mean about my insistence on *things*. My things are always, to my mind, more than themselves, but I do believe I have laid too much insistence upon them, and obscured the most important issues beneath them for my readers.

Legends, in other words, was her effort to deal with her critics and her self-doubt, demonstrating that she could write more about a world that thrived outside of her immediate perceptions. She wrote of attempting to capture the throb, misery and gusto of life as Lawrence had done, and "that is what I wish I could learn of you." Thus her letters to Lawrence were a way to explain herself as well as her aspiration to write as well as he did. Her compliments were not just throwaways, empty courtesies, and such.

What could Lawrence learn from Lowell? Not much, she thought, which is another reason why a visit from him seemed fraught with anxiety for her. She described her situation and misgivings in a letter (6 April 1923) sent to him in Mexico City:

> I see my little sunken garden flanked with clipped trees on both sides, and over the greenhouse past the shaven hedge, a road bordered by elm trees, a wide country road. I have been many times struck in looking at just that view, with its resemblance to a garden corner, and road beyond, I once saw in Liverpool. To be sure, these elms are American elms, and the shaven hedge is maplewood rather than box or privet, and the edges of my garden beds are of sea-thrift, not of lavender, but this place being laid out shortly after the Revolution, it was done "in the English taste," as the old garden books say. My house is definitely Georgian red brick. My library is panelled with English oak; so when you

come to see me, you will probably find yourself in the uninteresting surroundings of complete familiarity.

Lowell believed Lawrence was looking for an unruly, elemental world that her poems, if not her way of living, enacted. He surely had had enough of clipped and shaven worlds, the stultifying neatness of his native England. Better to carry on a correspondence outside the borders of her ordered world than to hazard his exposure to her daily regime.

By the summer of 1923, it was clear that Lawrence would not be able (or was not willing) to visit Lowell. Instead in one of his last letters to her he closed by saying, "But we'll keep a bit of decent kindliness at the bottom of our hearts, as we had ten years ago. I'll never let the world bankrupt me *quite* in this."

The *quite* is the essential word, because Lawrence did, at times, express harsh views of Lowell that have led certain critics and biographers to question the sincerity of his letters to her. After praising *Men, Women and Ghosts* in November 1916, he wrote to a friend that Lowell was "not a good poetess." Another letter refers to her as a "bitch." In still another in March 1920 he described her as "trying to keep afloat on the gas of her own importance: hard work considering her bulk." In September 1922, she is "a cupboard that loves itself. I'm glad that by sheer intuition I gave her a few slaps last time I wrote her. She goes off my list now."

None of these stray remarks, however, obliterate the record of a ten-year correspondence, and they have to be set beside Lawrence's other comments that Lowell was a "good friend" and a "good soul." It is telling, as well, that she never did go off his list. As E. Claire Healey and Keith Cushman, editors of the Lowell/Lawrence correspondence, observe: "Lawrence wrote his last letter to Lowell just five weeks before her death."

Lawrence could not *quite* forsake his "dear Amy"—in part, I suggest, precisely because she did not want to let go of him. She was always *there*, a *thing* that he could praise and blame as he liked, but always a figure on his side. She yearned for his approval, but she could live without it so long as he continued to acknowledge her. But for her persistent attention to him, who knows? Perhaps Lawrence would have let the correspondence lapse, although he wrote nearly three times as many letters to her as she did to him. The world was too much with Amy Lowell for D. H. Lawrence's taste, and yet as a soul who selected his own society, Lawrence could not *quite* do without her. It is perhaps as much of a tribute as she could have craved.

4

Wearing Well: Amy Lowell and Robert Frost

I intend to write this chapter not in the order of my reading but rather as a point-by-point investigation of how the friendship between Amy Lowell and Robert Frost developed. Imagine, then, my sources are lined up side-by-side so that I can flit between them, slowing building up an episode-by-episode narrative of their nexus.

In *Tendencies In Modern American Poetry*, which includes Lowell's most extended study of Frost, she recalls that while in England during the summer of 1914 she heard much talk of Frost's second volume of verse, *North of Boston*. The buzz about Frost intrigued her, and his work became part of what she described as a London "full of poets, and, what is better, the beliefs, and protests, and hates of poets. They made a lively buzzing which meant that the art was in a vigorous condition." Finding Frost in London was, in effect, what Lowell had come to London for. It is a point worth pondering because so many accounts concentrate on her ambition and desire to link herself with the new poetry as an act of self-promotion.

But Frost was not a new poet, and he was not claiming to be *new*—as Lowell herself reports: Instead of attaching himself to a clique of poets (as Lowell would do with the Imagists), Frost fenced with Pound and others but kept his own counsel. No matter how much the poets talked and parted and talked again (to paraphrase Lowell's evocation of the to-and-fro of these literary assignations) Frost kept himself aloof from "this clogging mist of discussion." He behaved, in other words, as the odd-man-out among the clubbable poets, and Lowell seemed to love him all the more for it:

> To anyone less firmly set on his own artistic feet than Mr. Frost, the situation was intoxicating but it is characteristic of the man that he lost neither his head nor his originality. He changed no whit in poetry, speech, or appearance. He talked and listened, and went home and did the same thing right over again only better. . . .

Not only did Lowell not decry his blank verse or deplore him as a sonneteer she seemed to positively revel in his deft deployment of conventional forms and lauded his subtle handling of iambs, anapests, and trochees. And why not? After all, she had written her share of sonnets and experimented with rhyme schemes while realizing that she had failed to produce distinguished work in her first book.

Lowell admired Frost for creating poetry that was at once so colloquial and yet so traditional in its meter. If she had found her voice by taking up the "new poetry," he had found his by withdrawing deeper into himself. As such, he remained a perpetual source of fascination for Lowell—as she made clear in her March 5, 1925 birthday tribute to him:

> Young poets are the most intolerant of human beings, and the little group with whom I had allied myself were quite certain that blank verse was an outworn medium, and that *le mot juste* was the most important factor of poetry. That night taught me a lesson which I have never forgotten. For here was our vaunted

most juste embedded in a blank verse so fresh, living, and original that nothing on the score of vividness and straightforward presentation—our shibboleths— could be brought against it.

However much Amy Lowell used the cause of poetry to serve herself, she never forgot her service to the cause of poetry that Frost embodied. Indeed, she idealized Frost as poetry's best self, an intuitive writer of great integrity—the very antithesis of a saloniste.

Lowell set the poet up almost in the fashion of Plutarch's parallel lives, comparing him to the intellectual Edwin Arlington Robinson:

> Mr. Robinson speculates about the world, wonders about it, almost agonizes over some of its phases; Mr. Frost, plastic and passive, permits the world to make upon him what imprint it will. Mr. Robinson is concerned that his work tally with the thing observed; Mr. Frost is anxious to trace accurately the markings burnt into the sensitive plate of his mind.

Quite aside from her judgments of particular poems and themes in Frost's work, Lowell presents him as a nonpareil.

After buying a copy of *North of Boston* in Harold Monro's Poetry Bookshop in the summer of 1914, Lowell took turns reading it with Ada Russell. Then Lowell left London determined to make Frost's name known in his native land. This is what Frost later learned about her enjoyment and promotion of his poetry. It is hard to believe, then, that he did not feel the extraordinary power of her generous tributes to him, or that she did not feel, in his presence, the extent of his gratitude to her.

But that is not how Frost's or Lowell's biographers see it—or even as Frost himself portrayed his friendship with Lowell.[17] Biographers often begin with the fact that initially Frost did not want to meet her. One can almost hear the sneer in his voice when he declared he had no need to meet the sister of Harvard's president when he had already met the president. Frost did not like Lowell's poetry, adds Lawrance Thompson, and so rejected Pound's offer to arrange a get-together when both poets were in London. Jean Gould has Frost expressing dismay over Lowell's "tactics" (presumably her brash maneuvers on behalf of herself and the new poetry) and Pound's boast, "When I get through with that girl, she'll think she was born in free verse."

Girl? Well, whatever else Pound or Frost thought of Lowell c. 1913-1914, clearly they deemed her an inferior. They thought in terms of a not-very-good poet blundering onto the London stage trading on her wealth and family connections and embracing the new poetry as the new fad. Vestiges of this view of Lowell as energetic, noisy, and pushy remain in books like *D. H. Lawrence and His World*, which reports that she "bustled into London" collecting poets. But her commitment to Frost, like her attachment to Lawrence, was a far more serious affair than these superficial glimpses disclose.

Lowell returned to the States and tried to persuade Houghton Mifflin to publish *North of Boston*. And when that move did not work, she did the next best thing: publishing a glowing notice of Frost's book in *The New Republic*. The review plainly reflected Lowell's goal: to find for Frost the largest possible audience.

Whatever reservations Frost might have about some of Lowell's judgments of him—he did not see himself as the bucolic pure soul who wrote about a degenerate New England—he recognized at once that she was on his side, a fact many of his biographers tend to obscure by larding Lowell with epithets. Thus Jeffrey Meyers dubs her the "literary field marshal of Boston." And here is how Lawrance Thompson describes Frost, visiting friends in Cambridge, putting in a call to thank Lowell for her *New Republic* review: "She responded with typical imperiousness. She was having a small dinner party three nights hence, she said, and he must be her guest on that occasion." That Lowell could be imperious cannot be gainsaid, but is this how, in this instance, she responded to Frost? Was she not merely expressing her enthusiasm over hearing from a poet she cherished and had shared with her loved one? Thompson treats Frost's call as a kind of obligation the poet feels he must perform. To be sure, but Jay Parini (always a antidote to the toxic Thompson/Meyers line) notes, ""The person he most wanted to meet was Amy Lowell . . . . [After telephoning her] she insisted that he come to dinner that evening at her mansion in Brookline." This is at least a more neutral way of describing the invitation, the tone of which, cannot now be reconstructed. However, nowhere in her subsequent dealings with Frost is there even a hint of anything other than profound respect for the man and the poet. Frost certainly liked the way she cosseted him and his wife Elinor, and his true feelings for Lowell would emerge not when playing the superior poet with Louis Untermeyer and Lawrance Thompson but—as we shall see—when he was acting as the sensitive father with his daughter Lesley.

Thompson, relying on what Frost told him and on Damon's biography, recounts Frost's approach to Sevenels, his braving of the seven rambunctious sheep dogs, and his trepidation at meeting his formidable hostess, and her surprisingly welcome manner: "He had been warned that she was a huge woman whose corpulence was caused by a glandular ailment, but he was quickly put at ease by the liveliness of her manner and the genuine cordiality of her welcome." Lowell lived in a sumptuous world (Thompson describes the grandeur of her library), but the biographer is forced to give her her down-to-earth due. After describing Lowell's tolerant listening to a boring Nicaraguan reciting his verse as Frost arrived, Thompson reports her verdict on the departing poet: a "derisive thumb-to-nose dismissal. Frost, delighted with the unexpected crudeness of the gesture, immediately decided that he and Miss Lowell would get along well, no matter how much they might disagree over the present state of New England or of poetry." Indeed, Frost was "thoroughly entertained by the raucous prejudices of his hostess."

Thompson mentions Lowell's diatribe against Harriet Monroe. Very likely. Lowell often groused about Monroe's treatment of her, since the latter was loathe to ever compliment the former on her work, even when it appeared in Monroe's *Poetry*. But then Thompson gets Lowell utterly wrong on the subject of Ezra Pound: "of course she wasn't prepared to have Ezra rewrite some of her poems to demonstrate that she hadn't yet mastered the principles of 'Imagisme.'" There is no evidence to support Thompson, and his misreporting is only worth comment as an example of the accumulating prejudice against Lowell that results in a view of her that has damaged her reputation. She was no prima donna concerning her own poetry—certainly not when she met Pound. She had one not-very-successful book to her credit and many doubts about her own talent, and Pound—whatever his qualms about her work—would hardly have treated her so roughly in personal meetings that he arranged in the hope of acquiring her financial support for his various schemes. Much of the bad blood between them flowed after she returned to the U. S. from her second trip to England and took with her the support of Pound's fellow Imagists in order to produce an edition of Imagist poetry stateside. In other words, Thompson, like many other biographers, loads up his portrayal of Lowell with all he thinks he knows about her, even though much of what he knows has no bearing on certain moments—especially the early ones—in her career as a poet.

Thus Thompson's belittling of Lowell tends to infect the way he describes Frost's entrance into her life: "Very few people were able to outtalk Robert Frost on occasions like this, but Amy Lowell did." Thompson mentions but does not seem to understand John Gould Fletcher's account of this first Lowell/Frost rendezvous: "I was struck by the Celtic dreaminess of his eyes, his quiet unworldliness, his serene detachment of manner. He sat on a sofa and said little." There may have been many reasons for Frost's reticence. After all, he was a guest in Lowell's home. He certainly understood this was Amy's show, and he was ambitious, diplomatic, and astute.

In her Frost biography, Jean Gould provides such a different account of the first Lowell/Frost encounter that I have to wonder if she made it up (her biography is largely silent on her sources): "He sparred good-naturedly with Amy on her pet theories, but when, after a cut-glass dinner, she lit one of her black cigars, blew a cloud of smoke and asked point-blank how he liked her poetry, he was at a loss to know what to say, since he didn't think much of it." So what did he say? Gould is silent. The cigars, by the way, were not black (a specimen is available for inspection in the Brown University library).

Like Thompson, Gould likes her Lowell epithets: "Amy Lowell's extravagant, regal officiousness rather amused him, and he could communicate with her on friendly terms . . ." Like many of Gould's sentences, this one seems to conflate later Lowell/Frost meetings with the first one. When Gould wrote her biography of Lowell, that first dinner with Frost took on a different complexion, more in line with Thompson and Damon: "aware that he [Frost] was more or less on trial, he was quiet, but by no means shy."

Jeffrey Meyers, writing long after Thompson and Gould, describes the first Lowell/Frost dinner with a veritable vortex of epithets: "Frost found the Gertrude Stein of Imagism obese, ambitious, domineering, egotistical, eccentric and emotionally deprived. Though good-natured, she combined execrable poetry with a patronizing manner and demanded constant flattery. Frost expressed his gratitude and was suitably charming and deferential. He made a favorable impression and left on good terms." Meyers seems to have overdosed on his sources, which is perhaps why he makes the dubious claim that Lowell was "emotionally deprived." Present at that first meal with Frost was Ada Russell, who had not only shared Lowell's enjoyment of Frost's poetry, but who had become Lowell's life partner. Countless witnesses testify to the emotional fulfillment Lowell derived from Russell's company, although Russell's behavior in Lowell's presence is rarely described or even mentioned. Not noticing Russell's beside Lowell, it becomes easy then for biographers like Meyers to treat Lowell's affective life in a vacuum. What is missing in most accounts of Lowell's encounters with Frost and others are the reaction shots—the way Lowell and Russell looked at one another. If a film of their interaction ever surfaced it might very well obliterate the narrow-minded narratives of Thompson, Meyers & Co.

It is said repeatedly that Frost disliked Lowell's poetry. Thompson reports that Frost found it pretentious. What to make, then, of this note to her after publication of *Sword Blades and Poppy Seed* (1914): "the great thing is that you and some of the rest of us have landed with both feet on all the little chipping poetry of awhile ago. We have busted 'em up as with cavalry. We have, we have, we have. Yes, I like your book. . . ." It is shrewdly crafted praise—mainly aimed at supporting Lowell's demolition of the genteel tradition. Like Frost, she brought greater realism of expression to American poetry, and so it cost little for Frost to side with her. Or is he simply indulging in flattery (that would be the Thompson/Meyers line of interpretation). Or a bit of both: some genuine admiration mixed with opportunism? To ask these questions is to enter the complex world of mixed motivations that reveals both Lowell and Frost engaged in a certain measure of devotion to one another rather than just using one to advance the cause of the other. How we can tell that Lowell meant more to Frost than is apparent in the standard accounts will be revealed anon.

The next Lowell/Frost encounter for which we have a record occurs after the sinking of the Lusitania. It is May 11, 1917, and Frost is excited by what Thompson calls "literary warfare." The poet is present at the organizational meeting of the new New England Poetry Club gathered to elect its officers. The instigators (Thompson's word) of this show are Lowell and William Braithwaite, an African American poet and influential editor who had praised her two volumes of poetry. Lowell had enlisted Braithwaite in her causes (including herself). At the moment, her plan was to set up Boston as a sphere of the New Poetry comparable to New York City. His own testimony suggests a far less brash Lowell and a rather vulnerable figure--hardly the sort to be called a "literary field marshal": "Nobody I am certain, pulled her out of so many depressions and discouragements during this period when she was fighting so hard to win the recognition and adulation she craved." Even if Braithwaite is exaggerating his role, his remarks present aspects of Lowell that fail to emerge in the biographies of Lowell and her contemporaries. If Lowell cultivated Braithwaite—bankrolling several of his publishing ventures—so did Robert Frost, who wanted access to Braithwaite's connections in the publishing world.

Whereas Thompson has Lowell spearheading the Poetry Club meeting, other accounts place both Frost and Lowell in Braithwaite's orbit as his allies. He was a taste-maker through his anthologies and reviews in the *Boston Evening Transcript*. There is no denying, however, that Lowell wanted the Poetry Club to make her president, or that she ran out of the meeting when it looked like the vote would be against her and in favor of a much more conventional poet, Josephine Peabody Marks, often called New England's foremost woman poet.

In tears, a tempestuous Lowell (sometimes the epithets seem inevitable) threatened to pull out of the Club if she did not get her prize. Braithwaite was able to broker a deal, naming Lowell as president and the older, ailing Marks as honorary president.

To be sure, Lowell was exhibiting her enormous ego, but then that is what was needed to push the movement forward. Without recognizing how completely Lowell identified herself with the vanguard overthrowing the outmoded conventions of a membership full of relics from the 19th century her behavior seems *only* egotistical. Note that with the avant garde Imagists she was quite willing to collaborate, but with reactionaries she could brook no compromise.

Lawrance Thompson depicts Frost as enraged over Lowell's treatment of him in *Tendencies in Modern American Poetry*. He was upset that he came second after Robinson in the book's contents, and he objected to Lowell's depiction of Elinor as a rather conventional helpmeet living through her husband's success. Elinor was nothing of the kind, Frost insisted, although his own portrayal of his wife makes her sound more aloof than was perhaps warranted, as if Frost were engaging in a sort of overcorrection of Lowell's profile. "What a cheap common unindividualized picture Amy makes of her," Frost wrote to Louis Untermeyer, the primary source of Thompson's account. Yet the letter to Untermeyer reveals that Frost—notorious for his attacks on his fellow poets—was hardly that aggrieved: "Amy is welcome to make me out anything she pleases. I have decided I like her and, since she likes me, anything she says will do so long as it is entertaining." This is a remarkably benign statement from a poet who deeply resented the attention other poets received. And as Meyers points out, Frost reacted badly to patronage and often turned on his benefactors. Although at one point he called Lowell a fraud, in the end he never deserted her. Indeed, it is hard to see why he wanted his daughter Lesley to visit Sevenels if he thought Lowell a fake.

Frost treated his daughter's first encounter with Amy Lowell as a kind of *rite of passage*—not merely as an obligatory call on a colleague he felt indebted to. He wanted Lesley to be at least somewhat familiar with Lowell's work—not a problem, really, since Lowell's poem, "Patterns," had become a favorite among the collegiate women of Lesley's generation. Apparently Frost felt he had to counsel patience: "Be fairer to her than some people have been to you. She's not going to examine you & see how well you like her. . . . She'll be interesting. You'll find there'll be a lot in what she says." In the event, Lesley did not meet a poet full of herself. Rather than an evening spent in talk about Lowell's poetry, Lesley discovered that all Lowell really wanted to discuss was John Keats. And this is not surprising—not only because of Lowell's dedication to Keats but because her treatment of Lesley was characteristic of the way she treated young people. She wanted to know all about them, to have their opinions, and to read their work—if they were poets.

But Frost could not be expected to know that the poet who loved arguing with him could be a different person in other contexts. He was much more comfortable dealing with Amy the impresario of poetry and public performer. Thus he laid it on thick in a letter to Louis Untermeyer when describing Lowell's visit to Ann Arbor and her performance in a series of poetry readings he had organized. Frost said Lowell seemed irked when he mentioned Untermeyer's comment that Lowell carried a lumber-yard on her shoulder, and she was equally put out with a janitor who warned against her use of her own lamp (it would blow a fuse). Then she made matters worse by treating one of Frost's students like a slave.

Lawrance Thompson builds on Frost's letter and later reminiscences to make her appear even more absurd:

> Frost had especially wanted her to appear in the series partly because she could be counted on to give a show which might ascend to genuine histrionics or descend to vaudeville. On stage, she was always a spectacle—stout, pompous, officious. When she appeared at Ann Arbor on the night of the fourth of May 1921, before an overflow audience of 2,500 people, in the Hill Auditorium, she was in fine spirits.

Frost enjoyed and exaggerated the high comedy, reporting to Untermeyer that Lowell had spilled a pitcher of water and then tripped over and ripped out the light cord so that the theater suddenly went dark. The poets and the audience seemed to enjoy the accident, with Frost playing up an audience member's shouted-out request that Lowell light up a cigar. Wouldn't they just want to see that? she remarked without affording them that pleasure. Thompson tops off the comedy by having Lowell return to form—at least to Thompson's idea of her form:

> Finally, when she could begin her talk, Miss Lowell announced with customary arrogance that she would spend what remained of the hour talking about herself, her theory of poetry, and her practice of it . . . she gave the effect of talking down to her listeners.

Lowell did, in fact, smoke one of her cigars, but in private, Frost records. That the whole affair might have been stressful for her and that she was all too aware that she could be made to seem the buffoon never occurred to Frost, who was having too much fun cutting her up. But he was too sensitive to her actual performance to remain quite so dismissive:

> Her speaking and reading went well considering the uproarious start she made with the lamp and water. I never heard such spontaneous shouts and laughter. Out in front she took it all well with plenty of talk offhand and so passed for a first class sport.

Note that Frost has to maintain his sense of superiority, a common enough feature when he was writing to a friend, especially someone like Untermeyer who was not Frost's equal but enjoyed his privileged position as confidant.

But was Frost right about what happened at the University of Michigan? In Damon's account, Frost is the clumsy one, spilling the water pitcher and tripping over the lamp cord. The janitor keeps Lowell waiting for a half hour and then, according to Gould, tells Lowell she cannot use her own lamp. Hence her frustration and irritability.

William H. Pritchard the only Frost biographer who regards the University of Michigan event with the proper skepticism, observes that his subject's account makes him "look like a sober fellow compared to his extravagant guest."

The Lowell who appears in Frost's account of her University of Michigan appearance seems so self-absorbed that it comes as a shock to read her shrewd sizing up of her host. In *A Critical Fable* she treats the poet as college-caught, a bird-in-a cage, "kept in a zoo." He had leased himself for part of each year to various colleges, making himself their "booty." The colleges had secured "a high atmosphere," even though it meant "violence done to his own special nature" for a "handful of students." She imagined Frost at the end of a school year escaping to the woods and hills. The subservient aspect of his position and her utter independence had to strike Frost with force when he read *A Critical Fable*. But biographers such as Jeffrey Meyers ignore the passages on Frost as college poet and instead suppose that her depiction of him as the "perfect cliché of a dreamy poet" was his main cause of action against her. Perhaps, but he had already tasted her treatment of him as bucolic mystic in *Tendencies in Modern American Poetry*. What surely bothered him more was Lowell's suggestion that he had demeaned himself by serving out those college terms. Lowell, on the other hand, showed up for her college talk and was not about to be bossed around by a janitor.

Jeffrey Meyers suggests that Frost eventually lost patience with Lowell. Yet he continued to visit Sevenels with Elinor, and Lowell certainly enjoyed their company, saying the Frosts "wear well." Frost supposedly was asserting himself when he decided not to attend a tribute dinner Lowell had arranged for herself. She had apparently called him up at 1 a.m. requesting that he and Untermeyer arrive early for her party so that she could tell them what to say about her. Frost had his wife Elinor pen a note saying her husband was too exhausted to appear at Lowell's birthday celebration. Parini calls Frost's refusal to attend Lowell's dinner spiteful. He did not realize how ill she was, although she took care to send him a splendid tribute for his own birthday gala.

Lowell died not so long after her 51st birthday, and by all accounts Frost felt guilty about not attending what would have been their last meeting. That he did not have genuine affection for her is hard to credit. But he could be malicious about her, and perhaps the memory of some of his harsher and hard-to-believe stories bothered him. Meyers reports, for example, that Frost resented Lowell's wealth and social position, which fostered, Frost implied, an inhumane temperament. He declared that he was going to bawl her out. But he did nothing of the sort, making sure to keep on good terms with her. Supposedly she told Frost that she killed her dogs because they interfered with her work, and yet because she loved them, she could not bear to part with them. Now she had a beloved cat but would probably kill it too. Frost responded: "I'm glad you don't love me." In fact, when Lowell did have her dogs put down, she was dealing with widespread shortages during the First World War. A lot of breeders put down entire kennels because they could not get proper food. As a result, many breeds almost went extinct.

A good deal has been written about Lowell's failure to take in the full measure of Frost's greatness. Indeed so, although the same might be said of Frost's evaluation of Lowell as a person and poet. Did he read her with care? When she died, he refrained from making great claims for her as a poet, confiding to Untermeyer that he had written some "compunctious prose to her ashes." His most memorable line about her-- "Her poetry was forever a clear resonant calling off of things seen"—is his view of the strength and weakness of her work. But as Jean Gould concludes, "Robert Frost did not realize the emotional value that flowers and all those 'things seen' had for Amy; nor, for all his insight, did he grasp her psyche."

5

The Big Blue Wave: Amy Lowell and Florence Ayscough

I

> In the spring of 1918, I was in Chicago and was talking to Carl Sandburg. I remarked that it was difficult to argue with Amy, that she was so quick and definite that she always had the best of it, and he answered:
> "Oh! Arguing with Amy is like arguing with a big blue wave."—"Reminiscences of Amy Lowell: Florence Ayscough to Ada Russell."[18]

Critics of Amy Lowell have often repeated the "big blue wave" remark without crediting its context. Ayscough was writing in 1925, shortly after Lowell's death, to Lowell's lover/companion, Ada Russell, who had become, as Ayscough liked to tell Amy, part of Florence's second family. Florence's letters to Amy often inquired about Ada and her children. Florence had been friends with Amy since the two of them were children, and Ada, in Florence's view, had given Amy the affection and allegiance that the demanding Amy craved. Indeed, Ada had broken the pattern of what Florence deemed

Amy's "foredoomed intimacies." It had all begun, Florence remembered, with her friend E. D., who "struck up a very intense intimacy with Amy."

Amy's friendships did not simply fail; they crashed. And so it had been with E. D. The self-described pacific Florence arranged a détente between the estranged pair, but they never resumed their former familiarity. The cause of this schism Florence could not recall, but Amy's reaction to the split-up remained for Florence a vivid memory of "how hurt Amy was, and how deeply she felt the whole episode. It seemed as if she could not endure such a breaking-up of what was to her a precious relation; and I could not comfort her, although she used to come and pour her heart out to me by the hour." Thus Florence and Amy drew closer together.

To the outside world, Amy Lowell was an intimidating figure. "Do you remember," Florence asked Ada, the incident in December 1924 when Amy had been late for one of Duse's last performances. Ada had argued with a woman who was occupying the seat reserved for Amy, and "you said quietly," Florence reminded Ada:

> "But I am very sure that the seat is Miss Lowell's."
> "Miss Lowell!!" exclaimed the woman, and she fled like a hare, never to be seen again.

Florence knew that Ada, an actress herself, would savor the scene because Amy's life was always such a drama. Indeed, that is what amused them about Amy; she entertained them. They regarded her robust and formidable persona with fondness and glee.

When Florence quoted Sandburg she was not complaining about Amy. On the contrary, to Florence her friend was a force of nature. Indeed, what others deplored in Amy, Florence and her friends relished: Amy made a spectacle of herself. Was Sandburg alluding to the image of a cresting blue wave that Katsushika Hokusai (1760-1849) depicted in wood block prints and that were published in the West in the late 19th century? Lowell herself liked to have fun with Hokusai:

> Being thirsty,
> I filled a cup with water,
> And behold!—Fuji-yama lay upon the water,
> Like a dropped leaf.[19]

Lowell loved the juxtaposition of the minute and the monumental, the miracle of perception the poet could bring to the mundane. It is what attracted her to Tu Fu, for example, China's greatest poet famous for linking everyday, domestic experiences with historic and public events. And Lowell loved to promote herself and poetry and the public enthusiasm for poetry all at once, finding grand vistas in common objects, and in the case of the Fuji-yama that lay upon the water, humoring herself with mock-biblical language suddenly made earthy in "Like a dropped leaf."

Sandburg and others might have felt engulfed by Lowell, but it was exhilarating for Florence and Ada to share her company. Florence remembered driving for miles through the woods, admiring Amy's expert handling of her horse and talking about "everything imaginable." Florence relied on her friend's "keen common sense and true sense of values." When Florence expressed interest in a "charming youth," Amy cautioned her: "never marry a man *unless you can't help it*." This response has often been cited as an example of Lowell's dogmatic temperament. But Florence concluded, "I cannot imagine better advice."

Florence, widowed once, and married a second time did not note whether Amy's advice proved sound because her marriages had been fortunate or not, but Florence was writing to Ada, a woman whose only marriage had been unhappy and had found her true love with Amy Lowell.

Early on, Amy had taken an interest in the "little girl from China," as Florence called herself. Florence was eleven when they first met, and in her early twenties when her family returned to China. Amy was excited about her friend's return to the Far East, especially since Amy's older brother, Percival, entertained her with stories about his travels in Japan and Korea. Every time Florence returned from China, Amy plied her with questions. "She loved to read and talk about China," Florence recalled, so that the collaboration of these two women, which began in 1917 and resulted in *Fir-Flower Tablets*, was hardly a surprise to either of them. Florence had been the one to first enlist Amy's aid in perfecting her translations of Chinese poetry. They worked amicably during Ayscough's visits to Lowell but also via correspondence, with Lowell constantly pressing Ayscough to meticulously assess her wording and phrasing. As Lowell explained in her preface to *Fir-Flower Tablets*, she insisted that Ayscough provide several alternative translations of poems, each designed to come as closely as possible to the original. This way Lowell felt she was approximating the poet's words without herself learning Chinese, a task that she thought would take a lifetime and leave her no opportunity to write her own verse. Although Lowell had strong opinions about her translations, she never dictated terms to Ayscough. "I cannot recall that in all the weaving-together of our dissimilar work a single hasty, to be regretted, word passed between us," Ayscough concluded.

That Ayscough may exaggerate the amity between herself and Lowell is likely, since she herself quotes Lowell's tribute and apology to her:

> You have been an angel to me—a monument of patience. I am not easy to work with, I know; I get so excited, and I think of the work and not at all of anyone's feelings. Forgive me for all my faults and

omissions, and please believe how grateful I am for your wonderful sympathy and understanding.

The Lowell/Ayscough alliance amounted to a climax in Lowell's lifelong interest in the Far East. The Lowell home treasured its Japanese prints and wood carvings, and Japanese art became one of the subjects meditated upon in *A Dome of Many-Coloured Glass*. D. H. Lawrence was quite wrong to regard Lowell's translations of Far Eastern poetry as some kind of affectation that wrested her away from her better poetic self. He liked to think of her as a Puritan through-and-through, an American original that had no business trifling with cultures alien to her. But what could be more American than this fascination with the East—as Emerson could have told Lawrence. The clarity, austerity, and image-making power of poets like Tu Fu naturally attracted Lowell. She did not live to execute her plan to devote a book to him after concluding her biography of John Keats.

Although Lowell overdid her belief in the fellowship of poets, which led her to make large claims for her ability to divine the purposes of Chinese poets, she understood well enough that she was projecting herself into the words of a language she could not translate, and renewing her own poetic vocation even as she was changing the terms of that Puritan inheritance that Lawrence believed was vital to her creative powers. As she put it in *A Critical Fable*:

> . . . the West is the East, with the puritan night
> Swelled up in a gush of approaching daylight
> At least, so our cherished delusion mistakes it,
> And since everything is as man's attitude makes it,
> What the Orient knew we are learning again.

In *A Critical Fable*, Lowell was quite capable of providing a satire of herself and an astringent commentary on her motivations and on others that is reminiscent of Byron's rhyming irony in *Don Juan*. She knew very well that she had created a self-serving image of the "East," making it an antidote to the darker, gloomier aspects of Puritanism that had haunted Hawthorne and subsequent generations of writers, but the "East" was also a repository of insight "we," not just she, were excited to recover. Hence the "gush of approaching daylight." She wanted to capture the overflow.

And yet Lowell's nuanced view of herself and her era has largely been buried in the welter of reviews and biographies that make her out to be the gorgon of modern poetry. By the mid-1940s, when the Lowell/Ayscough correspondence was published, the case against Lowell had hardened:

> Amy Lowell was self-centered to the extreme. She was incapable of sacrificing the smallest part of her "dream," which she projected far and wide, making the world an immense feast for her fancy. Chinese poetry was to her the most delicate of dishes, her collaboration with Florence Ayscough a means of justifying her approach to it.[20]

Lowell's gluttonous, overbearing figure disgusted certain reviewers of the Lowell/Ayscough correspondence. Thus Stewart Mitchell heaped up the epithets: "the belligerent character of Miss Lowell," who indulged in "a persistent perversity of pride," and relied on her "none-too-subtle pride of purse and position." He added, as well, a measure of contempt and condescension, referring to Lowell as the "spoiled spinster sister of the President of Harvard" and to Ayscough and Lowell as "diligent ladies." Mitchell showed real relish for his demolition by dragging out his derogatory words in the passive voice and then resorting to ridicule when he dismissed the "comical obsession of the firm of Ayscough and Lowell."[21]

Horace Gregory is hardly kinder to Lowell, considering her translations "flat and tame," and her work with Asycough as pure exploitation, the result of Ayscough being "swept into the tempest that surrounded her friend's activities." In spite of the evidence that Gregory himself accumulates to substantiate Lowell's lifelong interest in Far Eastern literature, the biographer persists in reducing the poet's effort to a desire to best Pound and another competitor, Witter Byner, in the field of Chinese translation. To Gregory, the project is not evidence of Lowell's keen wish to break new ground but rather a "fantastically laborious project" that had a "touch of madness in it."

Jean Gould brands *Fir-Flower Tablets* a failure, and even though she regards Ayscough as an "imposing figure" evidently worthy of collaboration with Lowell, Gould concludes (on the basis of what evidence she does not say) that Lowell knew the book was a mistake. This seems unlikely, however, since Lowell seemed quite avid over the prospect of another book with Ayscough concentrating on Tu Fu.

Not all commentary on Lowell, Ayscough, and *Fir-Flower Tablets* has been negative, of course. Their translations received a rave review in the *New York Times*,[22] and Kenneth Rexroth, a fine poet and translator, considered Lowell's translations her "finest work."[23] Even their rival, Arthur Waley, whom Lowell knew to be the best translator of Chinese verse, treated *Fir-Flower Tablets* with respect, if also with reservations.[24]

C. David Heymann, refers to the "thick-wristed, iron-lung efforts of the two ladies," although he notes that Waley praised her narrative and reflective poems. Heymann spends two pages on Pound's Chinese translations without even inspecting Lowell's better efforts, especially Tu Fu's "The Thatched House Unroofed by an Autumn Gale," which Waley termed "splendid." Yet another evaluation did not rank Lowell's translations highly but suggested they inspired some of her finest mature poems published in her Pulitzer Prize winning volume, *What's O'Clock*. [25]

Part of what bothers critics about Lowell is that she never forgot the politics of poetry and that poets have to fight to get published *their way*. Why did she have to be so aggressive and self-promotional? Poetry was a kind of business to her, although that did not mean she did not also regard it as high art. If she tried to manipulate editors and publishers, it was because they were always attempting to manage her. A case in point was one of Lowell's favorite targets: Harriet Monroe.

"I had the most amusing experience with Harriet Monroe the other day," Lowell wrote to Ayscough on 25 June 1918. "She wrote and suggested that we should not write the poems in short lines, and I wrote back and sounded as learned as if I really knew something." Lowell liked to have her fun and was quite aware of when she was bluffing. And yet so often what she says and does is treated without the requisite irony and humor that she obviously brought to her own battles. Thus Lowell enjoyed Monroe's "hasty postcard" conceding Lowell's point. Quite aside from the issues involved, Amy Lowell simply relished giving Harriet a hard time. However hard Amy was on Harriet, Amy, by her own lights, pulled her punches. To Harriet's mollifying claim that her remarks were "thrown out 'for what they were worth'," Amy responded in her letter to Florence: "I felt like replying that 'when they were worth nothing, why throw them out at all,' but I refrained."

Both Lowell and Ayscough understood how intricate and problematic their translation enterprise had become, and how likely it was that they would make errors—even if, in the marketplace, so to speak—Lowell put on a brave face bordering on bravado. At any rate, she told Monroe that the primary concern was cadence, not length of line, and that Monroe would only receive poems for publication that had been worked over and agreed upon by Lowell and Ayscough and were the product of a joint effort at rendering the originals as perfectly as possible. "It is always well to take a high hand with Harriet," Amy assured Florence. To state the obvious: Lowell did not take a high hand with everyone. And yet the obvious requires elaboration precisely because Lowell's critics see her only as an expostulating cartoon figure. *That* Amy Lowell is entirely absent from her correspondence with Ayscough as it is in her exchanges with D. H. Lawrence and others.

If Lowell erred, it was in the scale of her ambition—her conceit that a translation could, in fact, be nearly perfect. If Ezra Pound's translations have fared better among literary scholars it is, in part, because his work is more like variations on the original Chinese in Poundian terms. Lowell, on the other hand, attempted to suborn her talent in the service of the poem itself—a rather noble, if flawed enterprise. This, I think, is what disturbed D. H. Lawrence: Lowell did not put enough of herself into her Chinese poems. However, that she did achieve a certain success in Lowellian terms, will be observed in the sequel—when I examine her work vis à vis Pound.

Certainly Lowell's competitiveness—her desire to best Pound in the translation business—formed a part of her mixed motivations. She wanted to make Ezra and the "whole caboodle of them sit up" and realize "their translations are incorrect, inasmuch as they cannot read the language and are probably trusting to Japanese translators, who have not the feeling for Chinese that you have," she wrote to Ayscough. "I tell you we are a great team, Florence, and ought to do wonderful things." While several detractors have treated Ayscough as a Lowell minion, Ayscough's letters to Lowell belie that impression, and the latter fully acknowledged how dependent she was on her friend's expertise. To do justice to Lowell's ambition and her own sense of integrity, Ayscough studied with several Chinese scholars, using them to bolster her readings of the poems. It was tough going and Ayscough's modesty and honesty have been used against her by critics who sneer at her tentative command of Chinese. Waley thought Lowell could master Chinese in three years, a rather preposterous notion, and Lowell is hardly the first poet to work on translations of a language she had not mastered. Enough contemporary poets have worked successfully with collaborators to say that in itself the Lowell/Ayscough partnership was not a deterrent to producing good translations.

None of Lowell's biographers and few of her critics, it should now be apparent, have made the effort to show where she succeeded. And this failure, coupled with the unappealing image most of them present of Lowell, results in the burial of her best work. Like Eugene O'Neill, a great playwright who wrote many bad plays, Lowell has yet to emerge out of the detritus of her career. The massive quantity of her verse has immobilized critical opinion. And it is time to exert some discrimination, to implement a critical method that does more than compare Lowell's weaker poems with Pound's masterpieces, or abandon attention to her stronger poems because they may rank lower than Waley's. What, in her own terms, did Lowell accomplish, and how did her most successful Chinese poems lead the way to her final and, in many case, finest poems?

The blinkered reception of Lowell's *Fir-Flower Tablets* is apparent from reading Mari Yoshihara's "Putting on the Voice of the Orient: Gender and Sexuality in Amy Lowell's 'Asian' Poetry."[26] Absent from Yoshihara's discussion is the glutton looking to outdo Ezra Pound. Yoshihara's Lowell is not an isolated, monstrous ego out of her depth in dealing with Far Eastern verse. For one thing, Yoshihara provides historical context:[27]

> At the turn of the century, when the United States embarked upon full-fledged empire building in Asia and the Pacific Islands, the term *Asia* came to occupy an increasingly visible place in America's cultural vocabulary. The American engagement with Asia manifested in diverse cultural arenas ranging from

> material cultures and visual arts to performing arts, creating a culture of American orientalism. For women in particular, orientalism offered adventure, freedom, and empowerment that were unavailable in other realms of sociopolitical life.

In other words, orientalism became one means by which Lowell freed and empowered herself. This much is evident in her letters to Ayscough. Whereas many critics have seen her diatribes against scholars and sinologists as ignorant and arrogant posturing, her acerbity served to bolster her independence. Given her health and physique, not to mention her gender, Lowell could not command the world as men did. Her letters to Ayscough often report her physical agonies—mainly associated with the hernia that could not be repaired through numerous operations and that ultimately contributed to her death. Through Florence, however, Amy did travel the world. And the Ayscough Yoshihara presents—"one of the most important sinologists of the period"—is hardly the pathetic figure so many of Lowell's detractors portray. While most critics narrow in on the Lowell/Pound contrast, Yoshihara notes that Lowell's Chinese poems were part of a "burgeoning of translations of Chinese and Japanese texts."

It is rather astonishing that none of Lowell's critics read the letters between her and Ayscough as the marvelous duet that Lowell herself commented on in her preface to *Fir-Flower Tablets:* "Since neither of us pretended to any knowledge of the other's craft, our association has been a continuing augmenting pleasure." Even after the publication of *Fir-Flower Tablets*, when Lowell was deep into completing her biography of John Keats, she implored Ayscough not to send more Chinese poems because Lowell might very well be tempted away from the task at hand.

Lowell wrote to Florence Ayscough that she was thrilled when her friend, Professor John Livingstone Lowes told her how much he admired *Fir-Flower Tablets*, a judgment he elaborated in *Essays in Appreciation* (1936). There he extolled Lowell's sense of adventure and discovery, demonstrating how integral her Chinese poems were to her sense of herself and her vocation as a poet. To Lowes, the price of her poetry meant that she failed twice as often as she succeeded, and that she "sought and missed and won triumphantly experience and expression of those flashes of sudden beauty" which the less adventurous barely perceive let alone are able to articulate. She often overshot the mark, he conceded, but in the winnowing of time her best work would merit, he thought, "one rare and shining book." If such a book is ever to be assembled, it will have to include some distillation of *Fir-Flower Tablets*. It represents not a "mistake" but, as Yoshihara observes, "a woman such as Amy Lowell [who] did not miss this opportunity for new forms of expression."

Yoshihara sets passages from Lowell and Pound side-by-side, demonstrating the former's earnest efforts to capture a woman's voice—often a wife pining for her departed husband—in a style that emphasizes an exotic and antique relationship of the sexes. Compared to Lowell, Pound's version of the same voice is stripped of feminine signifiers and allusions to Chinese culture:

> [Lowell] At fifteen, I stopped frowning.
> I wanted to be with you, as dust with its ashes.
> I often thought that you were the faithful man who clung to the bridge-post,
> That I should never be obliged to ascend to the Looking-for-Husband Ledge.—Li Po, "Cha'ang Kan[28]

> [Pound] At fifteen, I stopped scowling,
> I desire my dust to be mingled with yours,
> Forever and forever and forever.
> Why should I climb the look out?[29]

As Yoshihara notes, Pound's version, titled as "The River-Merchant's Wife: A Letter," robs the original of its foreignness. His poem is spare and stark, his adjectives more concrete than Lowell's, making his "translation" more universal—that is less dependent on the Chinese original, and more familiar as a modernist work.

Lowell freely conceded the beauty of Pound's Chinese poems, but she believed he pursued an aesthetic strategy detrimental to the original poetry. In fact, Lowell's poem is much more discursive and letter-like in the length of its lines and its favoring of simile over metaphor. Less intense than Pound, her poem has, in compensation, a certain mystique. As Yoshihara points out, to understand the allusions to the faithful man clinging to the bridge-post and the "Looking-for-Husband Ledge," the reader would have to consult Ayscough's notes which explain the legends of the man refusing to leave the bridge where he is supposed to meet his beloved even as a flood drowns him and the woman who turned to stone on the banks of the Yangze River awaiting her husband's return. For Lowell, Li Po's poem had to retain its recondite nature for her contemporaries—or rather she wanted her readers to appreciate the differences between cultures that she and Ayscough were attempting to mediate. For Lowell, translation meant transferring the poem nearly intact from one culture to another. It was important to her to create a drama in which the Chinese wife regards her husband in the terms of her culture, seeing in him the representative of all she has been taught to hold dear. Such instances surely represent a heroic endeavor that ought to be appreciated in its own terms and not merely as a runner-up to Pound.[30]

II

> And everywhere, everywhere, there is poetry.—Amy Lowell, Introduction to *Diaries of Court Ladies of Old Japan*

Amy Lowell Among Her Contemporaries 95

Amy Lowell grew up with the Japanese prints her brother brought home from his travels in the Far East. Her introduction to *Diaries of Court Ladies of Old Japan* mentions the everyday importance of looking at those prints. What did they present to her? A world that was at once exotic and familiar, one she had never visited and yet was a fundamental part of her domestic universe, inspiring her imagination of a world "dowered with a rare and exquisite taste." These prints, in other words, were as much of an inheritance as her Puritan ancestry. She did not become a published poet until her mid-30s, but her aspiration to put poetry at the center of her life had begun much earlier as she learned of an old Japan that treated poetry as a "natural adjunct to every possible event."

The ubiquity of poetry in old Japan exhilarated her and motivated her efforts to make poetry count more with Americans. She yearned for a world in which court ladies wrote some of Japan's greatest literature even as "Europe was in the full blackness of her darkest ages," pursuing conquests with the "mailed fist" and massacres and in general engaging in futile and deluded dreams of hegemony: "King Canute was sitting in his armchair and giving orders to the sea." From the perspective of the civilized diaries European history seemed benighted and absurd: "And to think that even five hundred years later Columbus was sending letters into the interior of Cuba, addressed to the Emperor of Japan!"

Lowell was not merely engaging in a nostalgic longing for far-off paradise of poetry. She understood how crude in certain respects old Japan was—scientifically backward and prone to horrendous diseases and conflagrations. And yet the Japanese attention to color, so dear to Lowell's own poetry, drew her to the Asian ancients and a court life in which every cultivated person wrote verse and poems formed an important part of the betrothal ritual. Women in this world had powerful and enduring personalities. Describing the great diarist Izumi

Shikibu, Lowell could just as well have been offering a self-portrait:

> Life was powerless to mellow so vivid a personality; but neither could it subdue it. She gives us no suggestion of resignation. She lived intensely, as her Diary shows; she always had done so, and doubtless she always did. We see her as untamable, a genius compelled to follow her own inclinations. Difficult to deal with, maybe, like strong wine, but wonderfully stimulating.

Such writers are worth the trouble, Lowell suggests, and how could she not think of herself, and her own court at Sevenels?

For reasons of health alone, Lowell could never be the traveler her brother was. But she could bring other worlds home in her poetry, and she could impress herself on the world with her poetry, and coax her country to grant poetry its own province, if not the government of a whole society. What made Florence Ayscough so very dear to Amy Lowell was Florence's reach into the Far East. The idea that Florence was merely a pathetic adjunct to the demanding Amy is preposterous. Florence could actually go to places Amy could only dream of. Florence brought color to Amy's world, and stories—like the one about Hsieh T'ao, a courtesan "famous for her wit and verse writing," who "made a paper of ten colors which she dipped in a stream, and on it wrote her poems." This kind of fable enchanted Amy, especially because it, in turn, alluded to another incident years earlier in which a woman had stolen a stole from a Buddhist priest and had taken it to the same stream to wash it. As the stole touched the water, the stream filled with flowers, creating the medium in which Hsieh T'ao perfected poems that came to be called her "fir-flower tablets." This is a world in which nature and poetry are symbiotic, with poetry quite literally made out of the elements. This is the

Amy Lowell who treasured her brother's letters from Japan, 34 of them written on "washi," Japanese handmade paper. Amy Lowell could never make poetry this central to her own culture, but she could certainly die trying. Why Lowell's heart-breaking effort on behalf of poetry should have merited such ridicule and willful ignorance is one of the great shames of American literature.

Lowell's prose poem "Guns as Keys: And the Great Gate Swings,"[31] manifests her feelings for old Japan as a poetic land—first excited when she was nine years old by the tales of a Japanese diplomat her brother brought home to Sevenels. Her polyphonic work evokes Commodore Perry's visit to Japan, signaling the convergence of West and East, the opening up of a traditional society to Occidental trade. His paddle wheel steamer is portrayed as a contrary force to nature. Instead of relying on the wind, the ship sails in any weather in defiance of the elements: "How she throws the water off from her bows." This brassy industrialized expedition is juxtaposed to a scene in which a group of Japanese men engage in a futile effort to measure the girth of a huge pine tree by encircling it with their extended arms. Their hand clasps are repeatedly broken against the tree's rough bark. As different as this pre-industrial society seems, it is, no less than Perry's, dominated by man's urge to encompass nature. There is a poetry in their dance around the tree, just as there is an exhilarating power in Perry's paddle wheels that "churn her [the ship Mrs. *Mississippi*] at the rate of seven good knots!" Indeed, although Lowell is critiquing the brashness of American industrial might, she is also paying homage to it by personifying its inventions: "You are a proud lady, Mrs. *Mississippi*, curtseying down Chesapeake Bay, all a-flutter with red white and blue ribbons."

Lowell liked to provide elaborate justifications for her polyphonic prose, but "Guns as Keys" functions quite well according to the dictionary definition of polyphonic: "consisting of two or more largely independent melodic lines, parts, or voices that sound simultaneously." This is precisely what happens in the poem: Lowell gives separate voices to West and East, so that each in prose and free verse establishes its own melody, so to speak.

"Guns as Keys" beautifully blends the facts of history and the poetry of invention:

> Furnaces are burning good Cumberland coal at the rate of twenty-six tons per diem, and the paddle wheels turn round in an iris of spray. She noses her way through a wallowing sea; foots it, bit by bit, over the slanting wave slopes; pants along, thrust forward by her breathing furnaces, urged ahead by the wind draft flattening against her taut sails.

Lowell loved to describe things and was often criticized for her seemingly superficial delight in naming colors and limning actions to no particular purpose. But here, certainly, her vivid evocation of the steamer has a point: American ingenuity has unleashed the energy of that "good Cumberland coal," the good suggesting a sanctioned moral purpose coupled with an aesthetic outcome: the "iris of spray," signifying a rainbow of color, with the shoots of water resembling the long spearlike leaves of an iris. Like the ship, which is described as a living being with its own respiration, this passage breathes its own life through the intricate network of internal rhymes and alliteration: "Cumberland coal," "wheels . . . spray . . . way . . . wallowing . . . wind," not to mention the sibilance of "furnaces . . . six . . . wheels . . . iris . . . noses . . . sea . . . slanting . . . slopes . . . pants . . . thrusts . . . furnaces . . . sails." It seems nugatory to complain here that Lowell overdoes the polyphony since it is the main purpose of the passage to render the overdone, overwhelming force of modern technology, hissing in action like a steam engine that seems to triumph over nature. America is, in "Guns as Keys," a culture that overstates itself. It lacks the low-tech delicacy of the culture of "bobbing paper lanterns" and "glazed blue silk/Embroidered with nightingales" it is about to defile. The crudity of the American invasion is implied in a sailor's reference to the "monkey-men" and "little heathens."

Refined Old Japan is evoked in the spare free verse lines even as the bulkier polyphonic prose mimics American brawn. In the former, people wear "flower hats," play flutes, and walk on honey-gold streets while America sails the "seas of a planet to stock the shop counters at home."

On balance, Part I of "Guns as Keys," contrasts the robust American adventurers with the elegance of old Japan. But in Part II, old Japan is revealed as a creaking, cracking, decadent culture unable to defend itself or to formulate a plan for survival. A hasty, ineffectual flurry of fort building is no match for the "black ships," invading a colorful but effete traditional culture. American guns blow gaping holes in the corroding Great Gate. Lowell does not lament this antiquated land "with its five thousand men doing nothing with their spears and matchlocks." As fond as she is of Old Japan she refrains from sentimentalizing it, although she is hardly in a patriotic mood: "I wonder what the old yellow devils will do," muses Commodore Perry.

"Guns as Keys" ends on an enigmatic note, fifty years after Perry's Japanese conquest. A young Japanese man commits suicide on the high cliff of the Kegon Waterfall, decrying an unknowable universe and declaring "extreme pessimism and extreme optimism are one." If so, then as different as they are America and Japan are also one in what the young man deems the "infinite duration of Past and Present!" At the same time in America a "throng of people . . . Flux and flow through a great gateway." And the narrator speculates: "Debits -- credits? . . . Occident -- Orient – after fifty years." This ending seems a rebuke to both, East and

West, in so far as they have supposed their cultures remain intact and self-sufficient.

"Guns as Keys" explains as well as any Lowell poem her restless roaming of history and her attraction to exotic climes. Change is in the nature of the world, and Perry's conquest of Japan will result in transforming American culture as much as in altering Japan's. History is indeed a swinging gate—for both Japan and America.

6

Remembering Amy Lowell

I

In 1955, Houghton Mifflin published *The Complete Poetical Works of Amy Lowell*. While it was convenient to have all her work under one cover, the double column, small print, densely packed volume is hardly an inviting way to present a prolific and inventive poet.

Tiring to the eye, this collection included in larger print an introduction that was really, as Louis Untermeyer titled it, a memoir—in part a reprise of his 1939 autobiography, *From Another World*. His first paragraph set a regretful tone that seemed to sum up the reasons why Lowell had fallen from favor. He treated her as a phenomenon, asserting the virtual impossibility of separating the legendary and the real Amy Lowell, and arguing that she was "to a great extent the victim of her fabulous quest for novelty, and the legend of her inexhaustibility—a myth she herself accepted—[and] was probably responsible for her death." One can almost see him shaking his head in dismay as he perfected a picture of a self-destructive, out-of-control writer, subject to "drives which undid her" and beset by a "bewildering range of ideas and idioms, a constantly shifting kaleidoscope of style and subject matter."

Who was bewildered? Lowell or her readers? Both? Untermeyer conjured up a vision of a poet in chaos: "No one knows just how many poems she actually wrote, but some six hundred and fifty were published in eleven published volumes." Why present Lowell in such unattractive terms? Like many of her contemporaries, Untermeyer had flourished in Lowell's company even as he had to contend with her overbearing presence. It had been a relief to get rid of her because she was so wearing on the sensibility of less energetic and ambitious spirits.

Nevertheless, it would not be difficult to undo Untermeyer's first paragraph, noting that the way to separate the legend from the life is to read Lowell's best poetry that reveals her attention to craft and her unsparing revelation of quite intimate emotions that hardly square with the legend or myth that Untermeyer evokes. In other words, Lowell knew a good deal about herself and her impact on others--a point he could have shown by simply quoting the way she twitted herself in *A Critical Fable* as "more than a little volcanic,/ With a very strong dash of the ultra-tyrannnic." It is preposterous to suppose that Lowell did not understand the difference between the public persona she had created and the person who sat down to write her poems.

As to the legend of her inexhaustibility, Lowell would have laughed—wryly to be sure--at Untermeyer's conceit. By 1920, about mid-way in her jam-packed career that hardly lasted more than a decade, she was suffering from ailments that would cut short her life. She rarely commented directly on what others used to term her stoutness, but she certainly did not try to hide its attendant ailments or leave her friends in any doubt about how awful her exertions could make her feel. She persevered in heroic fashion, and without self-pity. In public, she engaged in bravado, to be sure. As Untermeyer reports, she told an editor of *The New York Tribune*, "I am as bad as Napoleon. I believe in my star." But in private, among those who really knew her, there could be no doubt as to what her dedication to writing cost her and how vulnerable it made her. After all, she confided to Untermeyer that his scornful review of her first published book of poetry had made her weep. Why didn't he present her as the protean writer she had become in an astonishingly short time? Why didn't he notice that her last work was better than ever and that unlike the path of many poets her trajectory—for all its digressions and dips in quality—went forward and upward. Amy Lowell's life and career was a tremendous success story and not the lamentable case study Untermeyer delivered in such a sorry fashion.

Untermeyer did not deny Lowell her historical importance, noting that after a conventional first book of verse her second, *Sword Blades and Poppy Seed*, had "sounded some of the first notes in the controversy which raged about the New Poetry. The book heralded the era's growing dissatisfaction with traditional measures and the determination to try new verse forms, strange cadences, and unfamiliar responses to standard sentiments." He potted up for the uninitiated Lowell family history and Amy's early life, although he focused mainly on mentioning her grandfather's cousin, James Russell Lowell ("wittiest of the New England poets"), and her brothers, ignoring that other aspect of her Lowell inheritance: a marked proclivity for doing well at business that was to serve her so well in negotiating book contracts and promoting her career.

Curiously he described Lowell as an "unusually pretty girl." The photographs show a pleasant enough and already plump young girl, but not the beauty Untermeyer describes. As to her "glandular disbalance" that turned her into an "abnormally fat woman," he took a comment of hers—that she was "a walking side-show" as reflecting a "mixture of self-pity and self-contempt." Maybe so, but this kind of self-reference is hard to gauge. When does the expression of a mood truly reflect a settled point of view? How Amy Lowell regarded her own body has also to be divined from the kind of poetry she wrote, some of which—especially the love lyrics—suggest a far more confident and less troubled person who enjoyed describing her beloved in such inspiring terms and with such sureness of possession that it has to be wondered whether Lowell's bulk got in her way quite as much as Untermeyer et. al. supposed. For Lowell writes not merely in praise of her lover but as a lover, a deft and skillful one judging by her vocabulary. When those writing about her poetry conjecture that it is only words, that Lowell was imagining what she in fact could not do as a lover, they express a kind of presumption for which there is no proof. Lowell's boldness broke new ground in poetry, and while we cannot say how she behaved in bed, there is *nothing* in her erotic verse to warrant the verdict that she was *only* imagining the physical act of love. Then, too, what of her partner, Ada Russell? She continued to live with Lowell to the end of Lowell's life and could not be in doubt that the love poems were addressed to her, or were about her, and nothing in Russell's behavior suggests the slightest embarrassment or recoil from her partner's passionate poetry.

In regard to that "monstrous distribution of flesh," which is the phrase Untermeyer uses when describing how he anticipated his first meeting with a 40-year-old Lowell, he does not seem to understand the value of his own testimony. He confesses his astonishment when the legend of Amy Lowell is countered by meeting her in person:

> What I was not prepared for was the extraordinary delicacy as well as the dignity of the woman. Instead of seeming a rakish masculine affectation, the cigar merely accentuated her essential femininity. . . . The disproportionate bulk was forgotten the moment she spoke, for the voice, half prim, half peremptory, drew attention to the tiny mouth, to the fastidiously fine features, the almost transparent porcelain skin, the quizzical but not unkind eyes. I noticed also the incongruously small hands and little ankles.

There is surely enough here to attract a lover. If Untermeyer could see and appreciate this much, how much more did Russell discover? Yet Untermeyer does not for a moment linger on what his own observations have to tell him. And that there was more to the Lowell the person than was observable in public Untermeyer observes when describing how "her working life was strict and severe" and that "everything possible was done to separate the private poet and the public person." Quite so. But then what of the Lowell who supposedly believed in her own legend? The public Lowell of the strident voice became in her meeting with Untermeyer a fine-featured woman with a "coolly modulated voice." She knew when to bully and when to blandish.

Untermeyer reprised her career as "propagandist and poet" without the sort of condescension of certain critics, although he implied that she worked up her own popularity by following trends: "When Japanese and Chinese poetry became a vogue, she turned a fashion into a lasting achievement with her 'adapted' *Fir-Flower Tablets*," failing to mention that her interest in the Orient began in childhood and that her period of extended work on Asian poetry began with prodding from her friend, Florence Ayscough. Sequence in biography matters. That others at the time were also beginning to translate Far Eastern literature stimulated an interest that was already well developed in Lowell.

Even at the height of her popularity and critical reputation, doubts were expressed, Untermeyer reports, as to whether Lowell was a great poet rather than just a "great personality." This either/or formulation has been part of Lowell's undoing. Her adroit buildup of herself invited harsh scrutiny after her death, when, it seemed, critics were eager to deflate her in a kind of payback for a presence that had been so powerful and domineering. No one of stature seemed prepared to perpetuate her reputation. Her work would have to survive on its own. Most writers suffer a decline in their literary standing and are forgotten. Lowell suffered a slow death as her work dropped out of anthologies.

If Lowell could be blamed for her own demise, Untermeyer does unwittingly provide an explanation. He notes that she was hostile to feminism—even rebuking Ruth Hale, an ardent advocate for the "new-fashioned woman" (as Lowell put it): "I believe . . . in the old-fashioned, conservative woman and all her limitations." Was Lowell merely provoking? Perhaps, although she shied away from any movement that singled out women. It would take an entirely new generation of feminist scholars to see beyond Lowell's seeming anti-feminism and through to a poetry that reveled in a woman's self-possession. Untermeyer simply uses the Hale incident as an example of Lowell's pugnacity.

Lowell was also out of tune with the radicalism that would sweep over much of the literary community in the thirties and that would make her seem a relic of another age, or what she called herself: "the last of the barons." Untermeyer reports her reaction to an anti-capitalism play (Gerhart Hauptmann's *The Weavers*), in which starving Silensian workers demolish not only their employer's machines but his home: "That is what is going to happen to me!" Lowell exclaimed. And, in a sense, it did, for she was caught in a kind of time warp that surviving friends and associates of hers had eluded. They had moved on.

Untermeyer is a case in point. His memoir does not quite compute; that is, he cannot reconcile the robust figure that dominated his era with the ailing woman he learned about only after her death, a handicapped person whose words he did not heed: "Keats is nearly killing me," she wrote to Untermeyer about her prodigious labor on her biography of the poet. "Do try and get here as early as possible before they have quite minced me to pieces and swept me up in the dustpan." He thought Lowell was joking. In his memoir, he felt compelled to confess he had no idea that she had to be continually patched up, suffering from a double hernia that was constantly threatening to split her in two. And yet this was no secret. Certainly Lowell wrote about it in letters to close friends like Florence Ayscough. If she had been more of a self-pitying person, Untermeyer would have realized her plight.

On one point, Untermeyer is unassailable: "Her final place in the history of American literature has not yet been determined." Still true. To his credit, he seemed skeptical about the cliché that she was a poet of surfaces and externals without much passion. In rebuttal, he noted that "succeeding generations have a habit of reversing contemporary estimates, and it is more than likely that she will be enthusiastically rediscovered." It is a pity, though, that he did not identify any of the poems on which this positive reassessment might rest. The best he could do was to avow that "her pioneering energy cleared the field of flabby accumulations and helped establish the fresh and free-searching poetry of our day."

And with that, the reader in left on his own to plow through the six hundred odd poems of the Untermeyer edition, bereft of Lowell's original prefaces and shorn of any commentary or notes.

II

It all seemed quite different in 1919 when Untermeyer included a chapter on Lowell in *The New Era in American Poetry*. He extolled her "amazing versatility" with a verve that is absent from the subdued mood of his memoir. Much taken with the polyphonic prose in *Can Grande's Castle*, he announced, "she has enriched English as well as American literature with a new and variable medium of expression." And yet 35 years later Untermeyer had hardly a word to say about this book and its inventive style.

In 1919, Untermeyer concluded his chapter on Lowell with this confident prediction: "When her collected works are some day appraised in a complete study of American poetry, it will be found that her vigor, matching her versatility, will have expressed that poet that is half-singer, half-scientist, and the groping, experimental period she helped represent." Although he still acknowledged her vigor and versatility in 1955, a much more wary Untermeyer no longer wanted to predict Lowell's place in American literature. The "half-scientist" terms refers, I believe, to his respect for her prosody. He extolled the technical proficiency of her verse as well as her balanced handling of cultures as different as America and Japan in "Guns as Keys: The Great Gate Swings." But this kind of praise and analysis was absent from his memoir. There his underplaying of Lowell's achievement reflects the decades of denigration that followed her death. No longer willing to make a case for Lowell, Untermeyer seemed only to be honoring a body of work—posterity make of it what it would was his apparent attitude.

Did the 1919 Untermeyer understood the full implications of Lowell's poems, especially the erotic ones, or was it just that he preferred not even to deal with the sexually explicit nature of poems such as "A Decade," celebrating her love for Ada Russell? He quotes the poem as an example of Lowell's "direct love songs" distinguished by "epigrammatic terseness and brevity of line." He calls the poem "excellently turned," passing over discussion of what the first two lines graphically portray: a woman brought to climax in a poem about a climax. The taste of love is relished for its own sake:

> When you came, you were like red wine and honey,
> And the taste of you burnt my mouth with its sweetness.

Critics had no language and no warrant for dealing with an eroticism so explicitly expressed. As a consequence, Lowell's full measure as a poet could hardly be assayed.

III

In *Poets and Their Art* (1926), Harriet Monroe divided her commentary on Lowell into two parts: the poet and the person. As to the first figure, Monroe chose to cherish Lowell mainly for her energy and, like Untermeyer, her versatility. But first the editor of *Poetry* magazine felt she had to put the poet in her place: "One may as well begin by granting Miss Lowell everything but genius." Lowell's "rich and strong personality," and a "character, aided by intelligence" made her one of those figures that "go a long way without genius."

Monroe attributed a good deal of Lowell's success to her heritage: "The force which Miss Lowell's New England ancestors put into founding and running cotton-mills, or belike into saving souls, she puts into conquering an art and making it express and serve her." Lowell was, in short, a "commander" and "organizer" with a "practicable literary talent."

As Amy admitted to Florence Ayscough, she often took a high hand with Harriet, and so it is no wonder that Monroe should salute the poet as a "daughter of the Caesars." The trouble is that the tensions between Monroe and Lowell led the former to see the latter as all brass. The quieter, sensitive Amy Lowell, eludes Monroe's attentions in an essay governed by sentences such as: "She delights in the rush and clatter of sounds, in the kaleidoscopic glitter of colors, even though the emotional or intellectual motive goes somewhat astray among them."

Monroe understood she was not quite fair, since she immediately lauded Lowell's exquisite "Venus Transiens" for its "fine precision and fragile beauty." But the editor quickly turned to *Can Grande's Castle* as evidently more representative of the tiring, hurtling verse and relentless internal rhyming and assonances that were off-putting. Although Monroe noticed the "delicacy" of Lowell's lyrics, the raucousness of the longer narrative poems apparently obscured for the editor a recognition of the poet's greatest accomplishment: her erotic work.

In "Memories of Amy Lowell," Monroe recalled how the poet had greeted the first appearance of *Poetry* with a check for a subscription "and a little more." Lowell wrote Monroe in approval of this new magazine's efforts to "foster poetry, which has a hard time to get itself published now."

At a banquet for President Lowell of Harvard, Monroe caught her first sight of Amy, a "ponderous and regal figure," descending a stairway and greeted by her brother's wife "in a voice which accepted resignedly anything that Amy might do." Lowell's first words to Monroe had to do with poems of hers the editor had not yet published: "Well, since you've taken 'em, why don't you print 'em?" With these words and introductions to others, Lowell had taken "possession of the occasion and the company—no one else was of any account." Monroe confessed that she was "duly impressed":

> So this mighty personage of august physique and fortune and lineage, sister of the president of Harvard, cousin of James Russell Lowell, was my correspondent, my poet-contributor, she of the beautiful handwriting and the meticulous precisions of taste in words and phrasing!

Monroe's use of "august physique" is intriguing, given the epithets like "monstrous distribution of flesh" that Untermeyer and others have employed. Lowell's air of authority was invested not only in her name and her reputation but in her presence, a power to attract—to hold the stage—so to speak that made her such a compelling performer. And though

Monroe does not quite say so, it is evident that Lowell was aware of her audience—or better yet—created an audience for herself:

> She literally sank into a chair, spreading herself comfortably and quizzing the crowd; doing not more than her share of talk, perhaps, but monopolizing much more than her share of attention.

So it was not merely by her talk that Lowell conquered, but like a good actress, she also put her power in an ability to listen and to engage others in the drama of her life by taking an interest in theirs. Monroe called her a "half-magnificent, half-humorous personality" because "there was always a laugh in her to confuse the magnificence." In other words, Lowell knew not to take herself too seriously. There is self-knowledge here of a very rare kind that most commentators on Lowell have lacked the grace or the wit to acknowledge.

So much emphasis has been put on Lowell as a self-promoter and publicity hound—and Monroe is no exception to this trend—that it is refreshing to be reminded of how Lowell reacted when a line of hers was dropped from a final proof so as to "slant the meaning of the sentence very disagreeably," Monroe reports:

> I shall never forget how the wires hummed because of this error. The poet's voice over the long-distance telephone was not angry—she kept her temper and did not blame the poor editor—but it was filled with anguish unutterable and was not to be consoled. From that time I realized to the utmost certain exactitudes in Amy's Lowell's taste and temperament which all her friends and business associates had to live up to.

Monroe then makes a compelling distinction between the person and the poet, one that others seldom observed or were too prejudiced to register:

> She might never arrive on time at a dinner and rarely even at one of her lectures, she might take it lightly when one of her beloved sheep-dogs chewed a poet-visitor's trousers and narrowly missed his flesh, she might revise at will certain other social formulae, but let an editor change a comma in one of her poems, or differ from her on a question of phrasing or rhythm, and said editor would be jammed down very effectively into a mood of proper deference.

Here is where Lowell's high hand struck—where her work and her career were concerned. Too many who experienced only this side of her assumed that this was all of her.

When Monroe next turns to Lowell's rivalry with Ezra Pound, she calls it a "pleasant enmity," a paradoxical characterization that she does not explain, although those familiar with the contest between Lowell and Pound know that on her side Lowell continued to admire Pound even as she felt he could not serve his fellow Imagists well, and on his side Pound deplored Amygism (what he deemed her low, demotic standards) and yet expressed no offense when she satirized him in "Astigmatism," a poem that dramatizes his dictatorial and narrow-minded methods.

Monroe witnessed Lowell on the platform and was able to elucidate the poet's appeal: "She was one of the few lecturers I have ever heard who could read a written address as effectively as if it were an extempore speech." The result was a "talk" that seemed both spontaneous and precise—without the hems and verbal pauses that break up the best of deliveries.

A dinner at Sevenels was a "stately repast," in Monroe's words, with Lowell "enthroned in a corner of the lounge," wishing to converse until three in the morning, a trial for visitors who did not practice her regime of working through the night and sleeping during the day. The entertaining took place in Lowell's library, evoked with marvelous exactitude worthy of Lowell's own quest for concision:

> She was an eager and delightful talker, indulging a discursive and experimental mind—a mind with much shrewdness and commonsense and whimsical humor under its more decorative impulses. And in that richly rusty old beautiful room, book-filled to the ceiling, she seemed completely at home with the forbears of her blood who had lived there, and of her intellect whom she could invoke from ten thousand volumes.

Amy was a Lowell on her own terms, taking possession of her family's past in ways that those forbears would not have approved. Their world had no place for such a woman, and Amy therefore had to re-create what an acceptable Lowell could be—much as her elder brother Percival (a role model for the new kind of Lowell) did for the male breed of his family. That Monroe saw no disjunction between Lowell and her forebears points to just how successful Amy had been in managing her inheritance.

Monroe returns to that word, exactitude, when describing Lowell's labor on her Keats biography. It is unusual, though not unprecedented, for a poet to be a biographer willing to subject herself, in this case, to the kind of minute details that have to be checked. A year before her death, Lowell confided to Monroe that work on the biography had worn her out. The poet was not exaggerating, although Monroe confesses she did not think that Lowell with her magnificent energy would die so soon.

Monroe does not call Lowell a great poet. How could she, given the analysis of Lowell's work that Monroe included in the same book? Instead, she pays tribute to Lowell's vital spirit, concluding: "She was a great woman, a true and loyal friend, and, in the finest sense of the phrase, a good sport." In other words, Lowell, for all the palaver about her dictatorial demeanor, was not, in fact, a party of one. Harriet Monroe, one of the great enablers of modern poetry, recognized that she and Lowell were in the same league, contributing to a life of the culture that was far greater than themselves. To lose sight of Lowell's integral role in modern poetry, and not to realize what a loss her person was to the cause of poetry, is to misconceive the history of her time—and ours.

IV

In *A Poet's Life: Seventy Years in a Changing World* (1938), Monroe had another go at Lowell, much of it reprising her earlier "Memories of Amy Lowell," although the added details round out a picture of the poet that has otherwise become all too fixed. Of her visit to Sevenels, for example, Monroe notes that "on the third morning, my hostess courteously broke into her hours of sleep by rising to say good-by before I departed for the ten-thirty train."

Monroe also added a gloss on her conclusion that Lowell was a "good sport" by quoting a Lowell letter that dealt with the editor's "hard-boiled indifference" to criticism, some of which came from Lowell herself. Noting that Monroe had managed to publish every significant poet of the younger generation, Lowell advised her: "So go on, my child, never mind any of us when we criticize." Monroe added: "however tenacious of her opinions," the poet was "always eager for arguments from the other side."

At the same time, Monroe conceded that Lowell did not think the editor rated her "at my true valuation." This was the Lowell who could feel aggrieved on her own account, wrote Monroe, who was still reluctant to consider Lowell a great poet.

Monroe criticized Lowell for leaving out Ezra Pound, T. S. Eliot, Vachel Lindsay, and others in *Tendencies in American Poetry*, a book shaped too much by the poet's personality and an inability to appreciate the development of American poetry except in terms of the six poets she favored. The book already seemed behind the times to Monroe. Certainly by the late 1930s Lowell's unwillingness to deal with a broader range of poets made her books of criticism seem even more dated. As a cultural figure then, she was losing her hold on a new generation of poets and critics—the changing world Monroe acknowledged in her book's subtitle.

V

Amy Lowell enters *Life is My Song* (1937), John Gould Fletcher's autobiography, by way of a story told to Fletcher about her disruptive visit to Constable, the British publisher that handled her first published book of poetry. An unhappy Lowell, on her first visit to England in June 1913, kept a taxi waiting two hours while the harried staff searched for copies of her book, which she demanded they produce before she would leave. When Fletcher told the story to Ezra Pound, Fletcher was surprised that his friend took offense and defended her: "I have already met Miss Lowell, and she is both generous and genuinely interested in modern poetry. I am to meet her again at the Berkeley Hotel in Picadilly, tomorrow night. Why don't you come along and see what she is like, for yourself?"

From Lowell's top floor apartment Fletcher watched her emerge in a "reddish-purple silk dress, with a high choker collar, cut in a style which was old-fashioned at the period of which I write." She had a "round pleasant face, equipped with eyeglasses and brown graying straight hair simply dressed, standing up around her forehead and fastened into a knot at the back" quite in the style of a high school English teacher who used to "electrify her class by remarking, apropos of some pointless answer by a student, 'That doesn't cut any ice with me at all.'"

Where Untermeyer saw a surprisingly feminine figure, Fletcher noted a "resolute and masculine determination." Fletcher remembered that after a six-course meal, he and Pound declined the large cigars she offered them, but she lit up one for herself after having cut the end with a cigar cutter at her elbow, explaining that her doctor said they were "good for her nerves." Large cigars? Perhaps if Lowell was trying a new brand. Her own favorites were small Manilas.

Pound discussed his theories of poetry, especially Imagism, submitting himself to Lowell's intense questioning. Fletcher liked her forthright manner and friendliness. She asked Pound to read some of his poems, mentioning she had just bought all of his books. After Pound read a few poems, Lowell said they had much in common, especially their liking of Browning. Fletcher confessed he felt left out as he watched Lowell focus on Pound. As Fletcher rose to leave, he surprised himself by blurting out that he would like to see her again and read her some of his poems. "Certainly, by all means," Lowell replied, setting a date. Fletcher's envy of Pound would be part of a pattern: Fletcher would often turn hostile in the company of others who were in Lowell's favor.

Compared to Pound, who took so much credit for ideas not entirely his, Lowell seemed open and impressionable but also independent minded. Fletcher felt he had a chance with her and an opportunity to detach himself from the Poundian agenda. Not only did Lowell respond well to Fletcher's reading of his work, she exclaimed, "Why, my dear boy, you have genius." The expression startled him—exactly why he did not say, except that no woman had ever called him "my dear boy." Fletcher's biographer, Ben F. Johnson III, suggests Lowell was taking a "maternal" interest in a young man twelve years her junior. Johnson also discounts another biographer's view that Lowell was "smitten" with Fletcher. Indeed, Johnson suggests that on the contrary Fletcher was attracted to a figure of "polysemous and dramatic" sexuality.[32] Just as likely Lowell was behaving as one of the boys, so to speak, affecting a chumminess confected with an air of authority that charmed Fletcher, who grumbled that Pound and his circle had certainly never been so impressed with him. Pound had promised to place some of Fletcher's poems with Harriet Monroe's journal, but Lowell was already talking about finding an American publisher for Fletcher's *Irradiations*, his recently completed book. Lowell was as good as her word, although Fletcher did not know that she was less effusive about his poems when she wrote to Harriet Monroe: "Queer as they are, they seem to show great originality."[33]

The lights of Piccadilly could be seen glowing from Lowell's long French windows as Fletcher talked about his latest poetry. He would like to orchestrate in words the vibrant modern city they could see from her apartment. He wanted to go beyond the Imagist concern with fragments (brief crisply described scenes) and integrate the entire city into his poetry. Fletcher, a man of nervous and tentative temperament, opened himself up to Lowell in ways he never had attempted with Pound & Co. Forming plans to meet her again, Fletcher departed at two in the morning, full of dreams of glory. He had found, in his biographer's words, an ideal mother figure who appeared to express unqualified approval of his writing.

From then on Fletcher's phone rang with Lowell's invitations for him to come to dinner. On their one outing, the taxi broke down, and only then did it strike him what an odd pair they made—when a group of "street urchins and solicitous street loafers swarmed around" them. "I began to be aware of the physical bulk of Miss Lowell, so much in contrast with my own marked leanness." Lowell had told him that she never dined out, and now he could see why. She had also told him that she never walked. So what to do? An uneasy Fletcher noticed that Lowell seemed "oblivious of the stares and the smiles of the onlookers, and, in fact, seemed to be rather enjoying the experience of attracting so much attention." There it is: although so many commentators on Lowell's obesity presume it was a burden for her, it was also a benefit for someone who wanted the weight of her presence recognized.

When the taxi managed to maneuver the couple within a block of Fletcher's apartments, Lowell "imperturbably got out" and they "walked resolutely around the final corner." The incident, Fletcher emphasized, was much harder on him than Lowell, an underweight man with legs that were "abnormally long in proportion to the rest of my body."

But Fletcher dressed so as to disguise as nearly as possible his odd figure. "Not so Miss Lowell," he observed:

> The old-fashioned cut of her clothes recalled the nineties; the mannish coats and stiff collars she affected emphasized her square-build masculinity; and her figure, to say the least, was constructed on principles entirely differed from mine.

In short, not only did Lowell not seem sensitive about her appearance, she dressed to be noticed. Untermeyer's rather more delicately constructed Lowell is nowhere on display in Fletcher's memoir.

Lowell loved the view of London from Fletcher's flat, praised his book collection, and, indeed, "admired all the details of my apartment with the gleeful avidity of a child."[34] Fletcher regarded Lowell's infectious enthusiasm as an antidote to Pound, who tended to patronize the young poet. Fletcher liked her deference to his generation, the way she would apologize for calling him "dear boy," although he admitted that "in many ways, her mind was actually far younger than mine."

Fletcher mistook Lowell in one respect when he remarked, "It was a mind that seemed to have lain long dormant, and which now, for the first time, was awakening: avid, greedy of sensation, fast becoming aware of its own possibilities." In fact, Lowell's first trip to London might better be regarded as the culmination of a ten-year plan to fashion herself into a significant poet. It was true she needed the galvanizing contact with Pound, Fletcher, and the other Imagists, but she was already determined to break away from the style of *A Dome of Many-Coloured Glass* and what Fletcher called the "cramping conventionalities of girlhood." He was quick—perhaps too quick—to see their kinship: "I, too, had but recently thrown off my own academic shackles, and had committed myself to the hazardous experience of 'Irradiations.'"

Fletcher, however, seemed dismayed that on her first visit to London, Lowell seemed so taken with Pound, whom Fletcher now regarded with some wariness because of his arguments with Pound over their theories of poetry. Lowell also had her disagreements with Pound, she told Fletcher, but, in Fletcher's words, she found Pound

> quite fair and open-minded as regards all modern and experimental work. . . . It was necessary, she felt, at this stage of the game, that all those who were modern and were writing the new, freer type of poetry should band together and not create needless quarrels.

Realizing that Lowell was not receptive to complaints about Pound, Fletcher decided to hold his peace. If he had done otherwise, he would likely have told her that Pound would never stand for such an inclusive notion of the "modern."

Not wishing to impede Lowell's enthusiasm, Fletcher did not argue with her about Pound but rather acceded to her importunate desire to read her new poems to him. They marked a "new stage" in her development she told him. Of the six poems he remembered her reciting, "The Precinct, Rochester," and "The Cyclists" stood out as expressing the "keen disillusionment" Fletcher, Pound, and other Americans felt about an England that was smug, rotting with inertia, and "emotional anemia." But Lowell's poems, Fletcher noted, were "sharper and more personal and more free than any which I commanded at that time.

"The Cyclists" is most explicit in its exposure of an England that is "dying" and "rotting/ Before time" whereas "The Precinct, Rochester" envelops the present in a historical continuum stretching from the image of an old Roman wall against which a pear tree ripens to those discontented people who would tear down the Cathedral and use its stained glass windows for their children's toys to the dean of the Cathedral perusing plans for its restoration and musing on how quiet and peaceful his garden is. Both poems are disturbing and pessimistic—perhaps inspired by Thomas Hardy, whom Lowell had just visited, although Fletcher does not make the connection.

"The Captured Goddess" echoed rather directly lines Fletcher had read to her during an earlier visit. They were part of a poem that Pound had rejected, but Fletcher decided not to say so, or to point out that Lowell was imitating him. He did, however, say that he thought their poetry contained similar ideas. But would Lowell have been surprised if Fletcher had spoken more directly? After all, he reports her as saying, "Of course I owe it all to you, dear boy."

The only discordant note occurred when Fletcher expressed his preference for Shelley over Keats. Fletcher extolled

> Shelley's magnificent use of symbolism in such a work as "Prometheus Unbound," together with his love of wild nature, that made him able to project

himself into every mood of a landscape, as well as his white-hot passion for perfection which was no less moral than aesthetic. Miss Lowell simply and sharply replied that Shelley was merely a freak and a cad; while Keats was of the great line of Chaucer and the Elizabethans. I preferred not to argue the matter, realizing that something in her puritanic upbringing had kept her aloof from Shelley's half-mystical and half-pagan pantheism, and that not a grain of this so-called "atheist's" search after God was in her practical New England nature. It was, however, an indication of that lack of sympathy which was later to develop between us, the first real rift in the lute of our concord.

Critics of Lowell have often recurred to her Puritan heritage when explaining her tastes and opinions. Yet such "explanations" seem facile and, in some instances, far fetched. Surely she had come to London, as her brother Perceval had journeyed to Japan, precisely to supplant that "puritanic upbringing." Fletcher reports that Lowell told him she was a "complete agnostic," finding little even in religious rituals that she could honor. Similarly, Lowell's refusal to make of poetry a kind of religion, to see in beauty a holiness—as Fletcher put it—he attributed to her "stubborn Yankee practicality and common sense."

Fletcher began writing to Lowell shortly after she returned to the United States in the late summer of 1913. Now he returned to his animus against Pound, claiming his *Des Imagistes* anthology was merely an effort to "boom" Richard Aldington. Indeed, Pound's behavior was a propos of "'artistic' 'literary' life as it is lived in London today," Fletcher wrote Lowell on 7 September 1913.[35] "A lot of tradesmen puffing each other's wares would be a better name for them.

I do not call such people artists. I call them dealers in self-advertisement." He wanted Lowell to renounce all of her recent English contacts: "Of all things on Earth, the most nauseating, the most abominable, is the London literary clique with its external politeness and internal petty jealousies and underground tactics." He even proposed that he and Lowell bankroll their own anthology. As much as Lowell admired Fletcher and wanted him in her fold, the shrewd Amy surely discounted the words of a captious man who could write in the same letter: "I am one of art's martyrs and mean to die in the last ditch." When Lowell showed no inclination to write off Pound, Fletcher followed up with another admonitory letter on 15 October 1913: "If I were you I wouldn't scruple to be a little high-handed with Ezra. You ought to know what is good in your work better than anyone else."

Sensibly, Lowell rarely acted on Fletcher's advice. By the early spring of 1914, he informed Lowell: "As you have surmised I have made up my differences with Pound and have even written an Imagist work." Fletcher was forever backtracking, withdrawing some intemperate comments, saying, for instance, in the same letter that earlier negative comments on her work were the result of "a very irritable frame of mind" so that he was "disinclined to be generous. I frequently am like that—especially in the winter."

With Fletcher and Pound temporarily reconciled Amy Lowell made her second trip to England in June 1914. In his autobiography, Fletcher makes it seem as though on Lowell's second London sojourn he observed a different person: a literary campaigner, although he did not "realize how extraordinary a combination of restless energy, thwarted ambition, and practical application to circumstances of the means at hand lay behind Miss Lowell's placid exterior." She seemed like a Yankee, and with

> uncanny insight of the old merchant princes of just such a city as her own native Boston, she crammed her own poetical shop from cellar to garret with the rarest and most exotic wares. Here was a glowing vase of Ming porcelain, there a piece of Venetian glass, here a gold and ivory fan from Japan, there a damascened sword blade from Toledo, here a narwhal tusk from the Artic, there an Aztec mask, or a piece of glowing tapestry from Peru.

She had her mind made up, Fletcher reports, as soon as she arrived in England to make of Imagism her cause—to the extent of backing poets and issuing anthologies. "She was convinced now that a great poetic renaissance in America was close at hand, and we could lead it if we would but hold together," she told Fletcher. He decided to sign on to her campaign. After all, on her first trip to London he had suggested they collaborate on an anthology without Pound's imprimatur. Fletcher admired her "bravado," the way she stood up to Pound when he declared that only he could edit an Imagist anthology. Pound's recalcitrance convinced Fletcher that he could not rely on him. And then Pound's crass performance (the bathtub scene) at a dinner Lowell hosted drove Fletcher even more firmly into her camp.

When Lowell returned home, she wrote to Fletcher enthusing about the "new poetry" movement. He should come and see for himself, which he did in November 1914, finding Lowell a generous hostess, dining with him at the St. Regis in New York City and then inviting him to Sevenels. He remained her guest for a week, taking a dim view of her autocratic style, muted somewhat by Ada Russell, warm-hearted, forebearing, and tactful—in short, a woman who had "lived long in the real world and dealt with real humanity." Fletcher never seems to have wondered why, then, Russell was so attracted to Lowell, whom he treated as far removed from common humanity because of her wealth.

Fletcher disapproved of the separate existence she seemed to live in her own house, never appearing downstairs before nightfall, and otherwise remaining in her rooms upstairs. The rest of the place seemed designed for showing off and entertaining. He resented the way she hid her Keats collection in a vault and was reluctant to have others handle her books (surely not a very remarkable trait among book collectors). She had even commanded him once to put back a Keats volume he had started to peruse.

Why these Lowell eccentricities mattered so much Fletcher never explained, and yet his stay at Sevenels unnerved him. Indeed, Lowell's attentions had exhausted the neuresthenic Fletcher, so that at a dinner in his honor he lashed out at his two male companions, called them gluttons (they had continued eating while he became feverish) and abruptly left their company, realizing too late that he had insulted the very people that Lowell had been at pains to introduce him to. Returning to Sevenels, he told a furious Lowell what he had done. She berated him "as if I were a schoolboy." Then like a schoolboy he "suddenly burst into tears—I did not want to stand there weeping before her and yet I could not stop myself." At this point Lowell softened and offered to phone her friends and tell them that he had gone to the dinner only to please her. She wanted also to send for a doctor, but Fletcher refused, saying he would write his apology to her friends.

What a curious incident. It reflects, of course, Fletcher's ambivalence about Lowell: his desire that she take care of him and his resentment of her ministrations on his behalf. Fletcher fumed that Lowell had kept him up late at night on her peculiar schedule. But surely Fletcher was annoyed with himself for feeling he had to please her—not to mention his unacknowledged pet peeve that she could never quite accommodate his yearning for her exclusive attention. The shrewd Lowell wondered about what Fletcher was not telling her. Why was he so wrought up? Was he in love? she pressed him. In fact he was and had been in a stew about Daisy Arbuthnot, a married woman who kept promising she would leave her husband for Fletcher (she eventually did). Finally, Fletcher did divulge to Lowell his troubled affair, but his confiding in her did not do much to assuage his anxieties.

After departing from Sevenels, Fletcher wrote Lowell on 22 December 1914, acknowledging her steadying influence on him:

> Do take good care of your health. Remember that I want to see you again, not as a wreck, but as your own self. You don't know how much it means to me—particularly since that night I relapsed and broke down—to have somebody who cares as much for poetry, and for me, as you do.

This Fletcher is absent from his autobiography.

Fletcher's biographer suggests Lowell pined for Fletcher and that some kind of sexual current operated between the two. He quotes Ezra Pound's letter to Harriet Monroe reporting that William Carlos Williams had told him, "Amy is roaring around a great deal. He also says that she and Fletcher are to be united in wed-lock, but this seems too perfect a consummation for me to believe without further testimony."[36] Pound's comment cannot be taken seriously. Lowell had other young men about her like Louis Untermeyer and her future biographer, Foster Damon, and made a habit of calling on them and making sure they remained in her orbit. She would not have liked the idea of Fletcher straying too far from the fold.

Fletcher was at least as possessive as Lowell. He was jealous of the Untermeyers, Louis and Jean, a couple of her protégés that Lowell especially wanted him to please. More than his "moody capriciousness"[37] emerged when he greeted them in a sulk. He did not like Untermeyer's leftist politics, and for some reason regarded Untermeyer's parodies of other poets as proof this was a man he could not trust. Fletcher also thought worse of Lowell for associating with the likes of an Untermeyer just to have another recruit for her circle. Sitting in a car Lowell had ordered for Fletcher and the Untermeyers—both dressed in gaudy evening clothes, according to Fletcher—he fell silent as the vehicle approached Beacon Hill and let Louis do the talking, making Louis seem in Fletcher's autobiography a rather insincere and ingratiating type.

Both Louis and Jean Untermeyer took exception to Fletcher's account in their own autobiographies, pointing out that they did not have money to spend on ostentatious clothing—indeed much of Jean's garb was homemade. And what exactly had Louis *said* that so annoyed Fletcher? The Untermeyers could not make it out.

Not even Fletcher's biographer seems to have grasped the obvious. Fletcher, an anti-Semite and racist, could not abide these New York Jews and was aghast that the aristocratic Lowell should find them so amusing and sympathetic. Most people found Louis's patter engaging, if a little overwhelming. Siegried Sasson, on a trip to the U. S. right after World War I, encountered a "voluble and exuberant personality which sometimes left me a bit dizzy." Untermeyer enjoyed meeting new poets and was delighted to talk with Fletcher. As Sassoon put it, Untermeyer's "receptivity was prodigious." But Louis could also seem callow: "He was refreshingly buoyant, and his smart-minded immaturity was preferable to pedantry."[38] Fletcher, much narrower in spirit than Sassoon and suspicious, invented a couple to suit his prejudices. He could never quite grasp how catholic and welcoming Lowell was in forming her circle of new poets.

In the later stages of their relationship, Fletcher saw Lowell harden as attacks on her and the Imagists increased: "The arrogant, autocratic side of her nature was henceforward deepened and intensified; and deepened and intensified also was her technical virtuosity, often at the expense of manifest sincerity of feeling. Her poems became and remained, more and more, "external" attempts to register a certain effect," he wrote in his autobiography. In private, he accused Lowell of treachery in maneuvering him away from Pound: "I regret to say that she pulled the wool over my eyes in this instance (as the saying goes). She has a very conniving way with her and she can persuade people better than anyone I ever met."[39] By July 1917, he had befriended Conrad Aiken, a Lowell detractor, and wrote: "I quite agree with you about Amy Lowell. She has quite gone to pieces—wreckage and ruin absolute. So vanishes another illusion of my youth." He could no longer take her seriously as a poet.

Fletcher thought that by becoming the point person for Imagism Lowell ensured a certain reputation as a freak and an eccentric. And she too often supplied what was demanded of her: a showiness and pyrotechnics that led to a "brilliance of surface" but not much depth. Both the poet and the person seem to have worn Fletcher out. He writes in his autobiography that after publication of the second Imagist volume in 1918 he wearied of her and "longed to get away into a more congenial mental climate, away from all this public lecturing and publicity-seeking in Boston, to face the problem of my own direction afresh." Lowell continued to write to him and support his work, although now abjuring him to keep his distance from Alfred Kreymborg and others she regarded as competing with the Imagists. Her letters made Fletcher withdraw from her further, since he now regarded her efforts on behalf of Imagism as mostly a way of promoting herself. Even so, he published a "wildly enthusiastic" review of *Men, Women and Ghosts*, which he deemed "rich, tragic, sumptuous, aristocratic, romantic, vivid and proud."

Then Lowell enraged Fletcher. When asked for her opinion, she had told Houghton Mifflin, then considering publishing a collection of his poems, that "though she did not like them so well as the others I had already published, she thought they would sell better." To Fletcher, she wrote that she was sorry if she had said "anything to lead them to reject those poems." Fletcher believed that Lowell had acted out of annoyance that he had left her circle, and in anger he sent a letter accusing her of stabbing him in the back. Lowell replied offering to bring out his book at her own expense. To Conrad Aiken, Fletcher called her actions "a characteristically Lowell trick."[40] Fletcher rejected her help, although later he admitted that H. D., Harriet Monroe, and others had shared Lowell's opinion of his poems. But he decided he could never be friends with Lowell again "on the old footing," and he determined therefore to stand on his own.

Fletcher seemed to be looking for an excuse to break with Lowell as a way to assert his independence. As Louis Untermeyer noted in *From Another World*, "Yet her most admiring friends could not help but resent her assumption of power, even when it was exercised in their behalf." At least twice Fletcher had asked her for money, which she sent him, and on a trip to Chicago he had acted as a quasi-spy for her, sizing up Harriet Monroe and others and providing Lowell with chatty accounts of their behavior (none of this is reported in his autobiography). He behaved, in other words, as a lackey—or at the very least as an ingratiating ally and then felt compelled to act the injured party in order to relieve himself of responsibility for subservient behavior that only abetted Lowell's modus operandi. Certainly, Lowell had repaid his service to her by announcing in *Tendencies in Modern American Poetry* that he was a more original poet than Rimbaud, and had a "finer ear." By 1920, Fletcher had published a damning assessment of Lowell's work, dismissing it as "purely surface," the product of a "rampant prosperity." This is one of the conventional charges against Lowell, but in Fletcher's case it seems also to be an effort at exorcism. On 29 April 1920, he wrote to Aiken again: "My own special hatred is Amy Lowell (that adroit pasticheur who once took me in—never again!)"

Fletcher visited Lowell one more time—in 1921—at her Brookline home. She was a "public institution," festooned with honorary degrees but also a "sick woman, existing from operation to operation, and straining alike her brain and her eyesight in her search for wider and wider historical perspectives on which to exercise her brilliant and panoramic and, at bottom, fatalistically decorative art." He remembered Ada Russell, "as ever, tactful and kind," showing him the wonderful Lowell gardens and others in the vicinity. His memory of Russell is rare among accounts of Lowell:

> I decided now that, of the two ladies who alike inhabited Sevenels, Mrs. Russell was the more appreciative and the more sensitive. I was delighted to hear from her lips how, as the daughter of a pioneer English bookseller she had spent her early life in remote Utah among the Mormons, and how on an early trip to the East with her father the train had been halted for hours while a great herd of buffalo walked across the railroad track. She brought back to mind the distant pattern of an earlier, more heroic, more generous, more charitable, more vividly picturesque America than now existed. Amy was at best only the final and cosmopolitan stage of that kind of existence, making enormous publicity out of her attempt to restate it in the most vivid terms for posterity.

Although Fletcher acknowledged Lowell as the herald and embodiment of the new poetry, he also saw her as a relic of an old-fashioned predatory capitalistic system. She was worried about labor unrest, the strikes in two mill towns named after her family, and feared for her personal safety. She spoke of hiring guards to protect her home, "as I remember," Fletcher added, further diminishing her: "I had not suspected her previously of being so lacking in personal courage." Lowell read her poems to him, but he offered none of his in return, confessing in his autobiography that compared to her he felt like a failure.

Fletcher met Lowell for the last time in 1923. She was in New York City working at the Morgan Library on her Keats biography. He no longer felt any rapport with her and deplored the appearance of *A Critical Fable*, which lacked literary value. It was, in his view, a piece of self-advertising. He did not acknowledge in his autobiography that he had been one of her targets, a poet who could weary one with his "polychromatic verse," the emanation of a man mired in "boyhood imprisoned in wonder." An even more personal thrust emphasized his emotional immaturity and indecisiveness:

> You can work yourself up to a towering passion
> Over landscapes and peoples, but when you would fashion
> A love lyric—Puff! and the substance dissolves
> And melts out of your fingers. A thousand resolves
> To break through with yourself, to have done with objectives,
> Leave you still where you are, exploring perspectives.

Fletcher lacked Lowell's confidence and go-ahead mentality. He was always worried that Pound and others, including Lowell, were stealing his ideas and plagiarizing from his poems. She looked the same to him, "still the active eager student, still learning, still experimenting, so much and forever the practical woman of the world." But now he thought she was to be "pitied, not blamed, for having made her life what it was. He thought her intensive work on the Keats biography would kill her.

Lowell never broke with Fletcher—even sending him the two volumes of her Keats biography as a Christmas present and letting him know that she wanted to see him when she arrived in London to promote her book. Her sudden death stunned Fletcher—as it did others like Harriet Monroe who had often felt beleaguered by Lowell's brassy behavior but now missed her challenging, startling, and surprising presence, as Fletcher put it in a poem he wrote shortly after her death: "Whenever I think of you, I seem to hear bell-notes calling."

Among his contemporaries only Amy Lowell in London had helped Fletcher define himself as a poet:

> Eliot had won acceptance only by a process of deracination, and Pound had doubly expatriated himself by migrating permanently to Italy. But none of these enable me to get a perspective on myself, to see clearly just what function I myself was fulfilling by remaining in England. Miss Lowell, I felt, might have done so, had she come. But now that opportunity was lost, and I was left to wonder what kind of impression she would have made on the stolid and phlegmatic English, had her good fortune vouchsafed her one more opportunity to triumph.

This remarkable passage reveals how much more than a self-promoter Amy Lowell was, and what her vigor had meant to an entire generation of poets. He also realized that she had died at the height of her powers, producing her best poetry that gave promise of even better to come.

After Lowell's death, Fletcher wrote to John Cournos, one of those present at Pound's bathtub performance, that he "felt curiously relieved, as if something for which I was partly responsible, and did not care to be responsible for, had vanished at last." When Fletcher appeared at a memorial for Lowell at Keats House in London, his remarks were conspicuously reserved and even cold in their brevity and blandness.[41]

On 1 May 1929, Fletcher answered Foster Damon's request for an account of Fletcher's dealings with Lowell. Fletcher evidently felt duly bound to acknowledge that at Pound's urging he went and met her. He "liked Amy, as was natural. She had the art of bringing out the best side of her audience. . . . The thing that strikes me now about all this was her extraordinary receptiveness to suggestion." In one of those half-truthful ways that informants have of dealing with biographers, Fletcher put a mild face on his ambivalence: "I have always found her very likable, very affable, but as she grew older, she became less and less open to suggestion: she was determined on pursuing her own way, and no one had an influence over her for long." Much the same could be said of Fletcher, of course. The "business side" of her personality irritated him, he confessed, but he never leveled with Damon—or perhaps with himself. What, finally, did he think of Amy Lowell? Was she a fraud—the amateur poet he decried in his letters to Aiken—or something more? Noting that she cared little for modern painting but delighted in modern music, he ducked any further discussion, concluding "She was a strange blend of the conservative and the innovator." Reviewing Damon's biography, which appeared in 1936, Fletcher seems to have calmed down. He admitted that as a Southerner he distrusted her New England "merchant prince" background. If he remained doubtful about her experiments in prose and verse, he also expressed considerable respect for her literary prowess.[42]

It is only fair to the mercurial Fletcher, however, to quote what is perhaps his last considered judgment of Lowell, delivered on 14 May 1943 in a letter to James Franklin Lewis:

> I am very glad that your reading of "The Shadow," an early—1913 or 1914—Amy Lowell poem gave you

what is undoubtedly the real clue to her personality. As you say, she struggled for unattainable perfection of beauty—(those strange watches in the poem!), struggled against the barriers of her physical person (if she had not been unfortunately too fat from young womanhood on, she would undoubtedly attracted *many* men, for her *face* was regally handsome and her manner charming), struggled *against* all the social conventions that were all her position in Boston gave her. The famous "black cigars" (really a light brown) which are all most people remember of her were *one* aspect of her determination to be as different as possible from the Society Matron of her parents and brothers and sisters expected a female Lowell to be! I am very glad you see this—it casts a flood of light on what she really was—and makes her amazing craftsmanship, which you also note, all the more extraordinary—as a part of the same *personal protest* against the cheap and commonplace.

How difficult it still was for Fletcher to gauge the poet and the person and to see the affective life Lowell did enjoy, especially with Ada Russell, whom he could see only as a counterweight to Lowell rather than as her partner and lover. Lowell's exquisite craftsmanship was, no doubt, a sort of personal protest, as Fletcher suggests, but it was also, surely, the result of her liaison with Russell, a partnership that coincided with the arousal of Lowell's most productive years as a poet.

VI

Two memoirs by Elizabeth Shepley Sergeant and Jean Starr Untermeyer are so different from others I have read that they deserve a special place of honor in Amy Lowell's biography. By titling her piece, "Memory Sketch for a Biographer," Sergeant seemed quite intent on showing off an Amy Lowell that had no equivalent in other accounts of her. The wonder is that no biographer has capitalized on this extraordinary firsthand portrait, one that Untermeyer amplified in her own sensitive remembrance.

Sergeant, a journalist Lowell described as "one of my greatest friends,"[43] saw—as I do—that Lowell's life was a triumph over adversity, the story of a woman who had made herself attractive and adamantine. Thus Sergeant's first sentence anticipates her subject's strength born of the challenges she confronted: "Her handsome head, unflinching in its carriage, had much to reckon with." Here Lowell is presented in and for herself—not as a "Lowell," a wealthy woman, a poet on the make, and certainly not as the emotional cripple who appears in the biographies of others.

What was it that Lowell had to "reckon" with? "First," Sergeant answers, "a passionate and untrammeled heart." This comment reminds me of Ferris Greenslet's remark: "Somewhere within that face and form so closely resembling Holbein's Henry VIII was hidden a heart that the world and the critics missed."[44] Like Sergeant, Greenslet believed that there were layers to Lowell that her imposing physicality belied.

That impassioned heart is most on display in Lowell's love lyrics to Ada Russell, but it also is evident in Jean Starr Untermeyer's portrayal of a very sensitive woman whose openness was both the avenue to her greatest work as a poet and her vulnerability as a person. Fletcher with his trammeled heart mistook Lowell's full-throated enthusiasm for naivety or lack of experience instead of appreciating how she was absorbing the world even as he guarded himself against it. Lowell was always interested in the other side, in her opponents, and she relished Louis Untermeyer's parodies of her because they caught her distinctive voice, whereas the small-minded Fletcher could only see in them mockery and belittlement.

Notice that Lowell's maladies and obesity rank second in Sergeant's estimation of a "physical illness, disability, and a kind of fleshly discomfort that no woman could bear in youth without suffering self-consciousness, and the sense of a lost paradise." Put this way, Lowell's plight seems melancholic and wistful, the story of a woman prevented from enjoying a normal, carefree early life full of promise. Sergeant is quick, however, to segue to a rather startling affirmation: "Yet I doubt if I have known a maturity as full-flavoured and wholly sustaining as Amy Lowell's." Thus Sergeant dispels the tone of desperation and need for constant diversion that dogs most narratives of Lowell's life.

In Sergeant's account Lowell neither ignores nor simply overcomes her burdens but rather takes them on, so to speak, as an integral part of the personality and the work she creates: "Every twisted strand, every quirk in her destiny which earlier challenged normality and happiness, became woven into the warp and woof of a noble and dedicated career."

Rather than Lowell shaping herself according to fashion, which is what Untermeyer and others allege, Sergeant's Lowell proceeds in an organic way. Rather than the careerist poet of surfaces, Lowell emerges as whole and healthy artist. How Lowell would have cheered this portrayal. As she wrote about herself in *A Critical Fable*:

> Despite her traducers, there's always a heart
> Hid away in her poems for the seeking; impassioned
> Beneath silver surfaces cunningly fashioned
> To baffle coarse pryings, it waits for the touch
> Of a man who takes surfaces only as such.

The last line presents a paradox: To recognize the brilliant surfaces of Amy Lowell's poems is to also perceive that the surfaces cover far more than themselves.

Then comes the most iconoclastic claim for Lowell's life: "There was at last nothing she would have altered if she could, even her mortal shape." It is an astonishing sentence that overturns virtually all assessments of the poet's life. Surely Lowell wanted a better body? Else, why did she have the mirrors of her abodes covered so as not to remind her of her bulk? Why would she call herself a sideshow? Why admit, in another searing moment, that she was a "disease"? Yes, as Fletcher well knew, Lowell enjoyed the spectacle of herself. Even more important, she was able to attract the unstinting devotion of her lover/companion Ada Russell, and, finally, she found deep satisfaction in the company of other men and women, teasing and flirting with them, in such a successful way that, as Louis Untermeyer notes, her all-too-solid flesh no longer seemed freakish but was, in fact, forgotten. That she had her moments of self-loathing is not to say that she did not also cherish the figure she had impressed upon her world.

Sergeant's prose has to be quoted in order to capture the complexity of the person who became Amy Lowell, for in Sergeant's words the living Lowell—none too keen on her huge figure—indeed a critic of her own size nevertheless made of her physical appearance an edifying edifice:

> It was, you may be sure, her own keen, not too charitable eyes which, looking down through her glasses on a figure they could not admire, decreed that it should be encased in a trim uniform of rich dark satin, with stiff boned collar and undersleeves of net, and that it should become, with all its limitations, an adornment and enhancement of that great personage, Amy Lowell.

The grand ending of Sergeant's stately sentence, in which Sergeant names or rather announces her subject, mimics the development and regimen that resulted in "Amy Lowell."

The balanced antitheses of Sergeant's sentences are reminiscent of an eighteenth-century Johnsonian style—an appropriate way to describe Lowell whose talk and manner have often been compared to that of the British man of letters. Sergeant's psychology might be said to be eighteenth century as well; that is, she shows how Amy Lowell constructed her character as an achievement. Absent from Sergeant's account are the demons of childhood, the scarring of the psyche, that has Freudianized biography so much that biographers have assumed that Lowell suffered from some kind of grievous psychological damage. Sergeant does not so much deny Freudianism its day as she implies it is inadequate to her own memory of Lowell that she is sketching for posterity. The childhood pain is there; the self-torment is there. But it does not explain, Sergeant implies, the person and her behavior. Lowell was not the sum of her psychological complexes. Like Johnson, she was astringent—with herself and others—employing those "keen, not too charitable eyes." And what a resonant phrase—"not too charitable"—which suggests Lowell did exercise charity toward herself and others but, again like Johnson, not too much. Lowell was not about to feel sorry for herself, but instead she would cut a figure in the world, building on her bulk, so to speak, until it became a thing of greatness.

Fletcher pitied a Lowell holed up in Sevenels. To him, she was out of touch with reality. And he resented having to conform to her nocturnal schedule. Sergeant, on the other hand, saw the home as an extension of Lowell's strength: "The high, square, mansard-roofed, brown stone mansion where this poet was born . . . and died, might again, like her body, have been a prison rather than a principality, but for the exuberance of her vitality and the determination of her will. . . ." Whereas Fletcher saw a person terribly limited by her wealth and unable to deal with normal people and everyday obligations, a diva demanding that everyone conform to her whims, Sergeant saw a woman who had pursued her art notwithstanding the privileges of her family and position: "Those who have conquered poverty and obscurity in the service of an art cannot perhaps measure the fortitude of those who conquer riches, cushions, and conventions to the same end. . . ." Looking at Lowell from the outside, Fletcher and most others could only see an affluent person with no significant problems to overcome.

Perhaps this is why Sergeant acknowledges Lowell's social and politically conservative views. She was through and through a Lowell, yet without denying that heritage she became something else when Sergeant visited her at home:

> Yet when one drove up to the fine portal of Sevenels, in the green gloom of a summer evening, it was never to dine with the cousin of James Russell Lowell, or with the sister of the President of Harvard University, or, if one were a friend, to pay tribute to a celebrity. When the smiling Timothy had opened the door of the car and rung the polished silver bell, and one had entered that vast antlered hall, and sat down in the formal drawing-room where flowers and paintings bloomed in a soft light, it was always with the sense that this was the abode of an artist. A spirit that transcended the luxury and formality that the eye declared brooded over the scene. It was a zestful spirit, spontaneous, vitalizing, and suddenly it took shape in a voice. A voice high-pitched in timbre as the roof it emerged from, sonorously hallooing, summoning one up two flights of stairs to share the mystery of the bedchamber. . . .

Sergeant's account, notice, is a summary of many visits—not the one or two that Fletcher and others write about. Sergeant's memory is vaulted with the exhilaration she felt in the presence of the world and the person Amy Lowell had built for herself. Sergeant's is the memory of ascent that she has fun with in phrases like "the mystery of the bedchamber." Lowell was the princess in the tower, so to speak, and the poet in her aerie. She was the siren calling to Sergeant. It is a bit of a joke, of course—Sergeant's big buildup to Lowell's entrance into the memoir, but it is also a splendid re-creation of how much fun it could be to visit Lowell and partake in the drama of her life.

Sergeant was not alone in experiencing the afflatus of Amy Lowell. When Foster Damon first met Amy Lowell, he was an undergraduate and had just written a prize essay about her. In person, she dazzled him, and he wrote about the encounter to a friend, calling her the "divine Amy." He wrote as if under a spell. Sergeant wrote in soaring prose in tribute to her own sense of ennoblement.

I suppose that Sergeant's memoir, and my redaction of it, can be accused of sentimentality, idealization, and, in general, an aggrandizing of Amy Lowell. But it seems to me that this mythologizing evokes the poet's attractiveness that is so often missing in other memoirs of her. As she herself proclaimed in *A Critical Fable*, she was the Buffalo Bill of American poetry, "broncho-busting with rainbows."

Here is another passage from *A Critical Fable* that defines the spectrum of impressions of Lowell and her work from Fletcher to Sergeant, in which she compares her poetry to a prismatic sky, "outrageous with colour":

> . . . The effect is erratic
> And jarring to some, but to others ecstatic,
> Depending, of course, on the idiosyncratic
> Response of beholders. When you come to think of it
> A good deal is demanded of those on the brink of it
> To be caught in the skirts of a whirling afflatus
> One must not suppose is experienced gratis.

Lowell took too much out of Fletcher for him to return the favor, whereas others like Sergeant and the Untermeyers felt inspired. Louis, like Amy, was a huge popularizer of poetry, an avid and influential anthologist with a reputation among the general reading public that would, in fact, accrue more to his benefit than his own poetry.

Where Fletcher saw a woman sequestered and out of touch with reality, Sergeant saw an enchanting figure in a fairy tale:

> Her wide, low bedroom, opening off a wide low hall, and bursting with books like all the rest of the house, was the centre of her kingdom, and her wide, low bed was the very nucleus of this central cell; it had exactly sixteen pillows and was sunned and cooled by a couple of dormer-windows overlooking the sunken garden where, in summer, fireflies were sometimes seen to light their lamps along the cone-like, clipped evergreens before she left it for a dinner late and ever later. I have seen her reading in that bed under a black umbrella in the bright light of mid-afternoon, smoking, of course, the equally black cigar; I have seen her "making" it—as she did always with her own hands—at one a. m., the faithful Irish maid whom she adored and abused, standing by to plump the pillows.

The notion of a put-upon servant "standing by" is surely one reason why the picture of Amy Lowell did not go down so well in the 1930s and afterward. Yet the sight of this potentate making her own bed with the self-indulgent sixteen pillows is comical—and a nice complement to Sergeant's bathetic "mystery of the bedroom." The beautiful garden, the books, the windows—even nature itself—seem in service to Amy Lowell.

And it is all a nice set-up for Sergeant's next vignette of a woman resembling a Japanese court lady shorn of her jewelry, especially the rings that Lowell liked to see sparkling on her small, delicate fingers:

> Yet I loved her best in her unpanoplied moments, without her rings, without her pompadour and topknot, her hair in a little flat twist, her innocent blue dressing-gown, the style of which must have been determined at the age of sixteen . . . Her face at such moments was candid too; Amy Lowell *en déshabillé* was a New England vestal, despite the colossal tiled bath-room that marked her a sybaritic empress, and the manuscript volumes, neatly typed by the secretaries, that piled themselves on the mahogany centre-table to make her a genius; despite the stream of command, vituperation, and imperious affection—redeemed all three from portentousness or sting by the flashes of Johnsonian humour and the warm radiation that carried them . . .

The foregoing is reminiscent of Boswell's portrayal of Johnson at home, his wig askew and his socks dropping around his ankles. The innocence and virginity evoked in this passage recalls the eager Lowell who first came to visit Fletcher, a woman so ingenuous that she could play the ingénue to Fletcher's already world-weary role, even though she was more than a decade older than him. He found it hard to reconcile the Empress of Sevenels with the woman who had come in learn from him at his London flat. Sergeant, on the other hand, reveled l in her friend's paradoxical personality, wonderfully captured in the locution, "imperious affection." Lowell was not two persons in Sergeant's view but rather an organic whole, and thus Sevenels, for example, was a "great old house which became a true extension of herself, as necessary to her as the shell to the turtle."

Sergeant makes no apologies for the Lowell that commandeered the world:

> Her real predilection, she declared, was for a society of slaves. Lacking that, she managed to enslave, not by ignoble means but with bonds of solid affection, all those whose lives touched hers: editors, publishers, reviewers, columnists, cooks, waiters, chauffeurs, human beings who brought stimulus and solace to her leisure, power to her various strenuous pursuits; masculine peers and feminine rivals in the fields of poetry, criticism, book collecting; and all the hosts of youth.

As friends like Foster Damon and Sergeant could vouchsafe, however, Lowell was hardly the out-of-touch figure preoccupied only with her own projects that Fletcher depicted:

> Yet she was a loyal friend and true, who respected and wanted strong characters about her—not just cushions for her ease--and got them, too. . . . how often did she dedicate her precious night-watches to reading and commenting upon the verses of some young gentleman in or out of college, some poetic duckling who might or might not turn into a swan!

Lowell had her measure of professional jealousy, but it was openly expressed when it came to her rivals in poetry, Sergeant notes, as well as being an aspect of "that eighteenth-century gusto for meeting and defeating others in talk."

Sergeant knew she was describing a period that ended with Lowell. Her death, Sergeant wrote, was like the fall of a dynasty. Sergeant worried what biographers would make of Lowell:

> My prayer is that she will find a biographer with as big a heart as her own, who will deal with her honestly, unsentimentally, discerningly, but not at all as Strachey dealt with Florence Nightingale or Nicolson with Byron. It would be very easy for some smart young person t puncture her soap--bubble of fame.

Sergeant worried, in other words, that Lowell would become the victim of anti-heroic biography—a fear well justified. Clement Wood and Horace Gregory did their share of puncturing, and even the sympathetic Damon did her precious little good because he was so gentlemanly and eschewed dealing frankly with her faults in ways that would appeal to a later age. Even Jean Gould—in some ways a discerning biographer—nevertheless labored under the burden of the negative biography that had preceded hers.

Rather than lamenting Lowell's lapses, Sergeant took her friend all-in-all, asserting:

> [T]he really intriguing thing about the odd scheme of her existence is that *it worked*. Amy Lowell accomplished ten times as much in the last fifteen years of her life as the rest of us in a half century, and there was no conflict, I believe, between her aims and pursuits. This was due in a great measure to the unselfish seconding and the stimulus which Mrs. Russell brought. But one never found the poet harassed and grumbling because book collecting and lectures intrude upon composition: she had time and

> vitality for everything, her public career served her poetic fame, her fame served her lectures, her collecting served her scholarship. They were reversible part of the same mechanism, and she was as much of an artist in the shifting of the gears as in the manipulation of words and poetic patterns.

It is hard to better Sergeant's shrewdly observed, firsthand testimony, except to point out that Ada Russell, who also received much credit from Fletcher, did more than assist Lowell or ameliorate Lowell's harsher qualities. What fun could that have been for Russell? And by all accounts Russell found her life with Lowell deeply satisfying. Why? Because Russell apparently understood that she was helping the poet complete herself. Russell was Lowell's gracious alter ego, providing a level of calm and even an antidote to her lover's everyday anxieties that Lowell did not merely benefit from but also, in a sense, created. As Lowell confessed to Florence Ayscough, she knew that she could be difficult and demanding, but as a team Ayscough and Lowell worked perfectly. The same is true for Lowell and Russell, who appears in "Madonna of the Evening Flowers" as Lowell's inspiration but also her reality-check:

> ALL day long I have been working
> Now I am tired.
> I call: "Where are you?"
> But there is only the oak tree rustling in the wind.
> The house is very quiet,
> The sun shines in on your books,
> On your scissors and thimble just put down,
> But you are not there.
> Suddenly I am lonely:
> Where are you?
> I go about searching.

This poem provides an insight into the way Lowell created her vision of Russell: All about her Lowell sees evidence of her lover's presence, and yet she is absent. A note of unease and urgency closes a stanza marked by the obsessional, "Where are you?" Work is fulfilling, but it cannot fill a life. Work is also exhausting, and the depleted poet feels bereft, perhaps even slightly alarmed because Russell has just departed in a kind of leave taking of life. All is at it should be (the sun shining on the books), except that there is no Russell.

Then the second stanza quite explodes with relief and exuberance:

> Then I see you,
> Standing under a spire of pale blue larkspur,
> With a basket of roses on your arm.
> You are cool, like silver,
> And you smile.
> I think the Canterbury bells are playing little tunes,
> You tell me that the peonies need spraying,
> That the columbines have overrun all bounds,
> That the pyrus japonica should be cut back and rounded.
> You tell me these things.
> But I look at you, heart of silver,
> White heart-flame of polished silver,
> Burning beneath the blue steeples of the larkspur,
> And I long to kneel instantly at your feet,
> While all about us peal the loud, sweet Te Deums of the Canterbury bells.

The religious symbolism is obvious. Russell is treated like a savior, and nature is turned into a church triumphant praising its Madonna. The smile is like a blessing, putting the poet in a state of beatitude. But Russell's mundane words belie the sacredness of Lowell's lines, turning the scene into a horticultural lecture. Russell, with her feet on the ground, so to speak, also brings Lowell back to earth from her spiritual reverie. And yet the poet's imagination, fired by her love, takes off again, as she does reverence to her lover.

Quite aside from the biographical implications of the poem, which Lowell had no trouble vouchsafing to her friend, John Livingston Lowes, "Madonna of the Evening Flowers" expresses Lowell's prowess with the love lyric. Because she knows quite well that she is idealizing the beloved, her unconquerable desire to do so becomes all the more real, an integral part of her ability to see the world as it is but also through the prism of her mind's eye. And this is what lovers do, of course, when they idealize the beloved. The poem is about that need to do so as much as it is about a specific individual's desires. The garden does need looking after, but it is also a manifestation of the human need to glorify and consecrate love. While the poet dwells on the heavenly aspects of her garden, her lover sees reasons to tidy up. It is an amusing and affecting encounter, with the poet refusing to give ground to practicality even as she has to agree the garden as been overrun—rather like the poet's own emotions. In biographical terms, Ada Russell knew how to cultivate Amy Lowell and to prune back her extravagance—a poet awash in her metaphors.

"Madonna of the Evening Flowers" is the importunate but also receptive Lowell. Notice that the second stanza is a direct address to the beloved: "You tell me these things." The poem is a dialogue in so far as its speaker wishes to share her feelings with her companion. Lowell's feelings, she tells Russell, are like the flowers overrunning the garden borders that Russell wants to restrain. Lowell's poem acknowledges Russell's role in the government of her life even as the poet insists on making her lover a figure worthy of adoration.

"Madonna of the Evening Flowers" is the best evidence we have that Fletcher's portrayal of a Lowell out of control is imperceptive. The poet was quite aware of her own extravagant tendencies, but both in her daily life and in her best work she realized an equilibrium that was beyond Fletcher's ken. Sergeant alone—except perhaps for Jean Starr Untermeyer— saw how successfully Lowell had secured herself in her union with Russell.

This passionate poem generates considerable heat, and yet the beloved is also extolled as cool and with a shimmering sort of beauty. And though Lowell has the urge to kneel before Russell, she restrains herself from doing so, implying a degree of self-control that is at odds with—and yet complements— the poem's own disciplined articulation of Lowell's anxiety and adulation.

VII

Jean Starr Untermeyer called Ada Russell an "equalizing influence" on Lowell, a woman accustomed to ordering servants to obey her "every whim." To read Untermeyer's memoir in tandem with her husband's is to recognize that Lowell was a somewhat different person with her female confidants, whom she brought right into her bedroom. Amy wanted to know all about Jean's life the minute Jean arrived at Sevenels, and this meant the exchange of much literary gossip and Amy's voluble account of her latest poem or discovery.

As ever, an apologetic Amy, the "solicitous hostess," released her guest "to go down to her comfortable room for a bath and a rest." Jean admired the same meticulous, aesthetic environment that Elizabeth Sergeant described: "One could see one's reflection in the highly waxed tables in the library; better still, one saw the reflection of the flowers, beautifully arranged wherever flowers could be placed." Everything that could be polished by hand or with buffers took on a mirrored brightness, the silvery sheen at the heart of "Madonna of the Evening Flowers." These surfaces—as Lowell insisted in *A*

Critical Fable—were the obverse of the depths she felt. This was not the ostentatious place that Fletcher rejected.

That Fletcher mistook the nature of Lowell's friendship is also apparent in Jean Untermeyer's point that although she could not praise Lowell's poems as highly as Lowell praised hers—many of which were published at Lowell's insistence—this made no difference in their close relationship. "Nor the fact that in other matters I disagreed with her." Untermeyer does not specify those "other matters," but it is likely that they involved politics. Lowell would not have agreed with the Untermeyers' New York liberalism, but unlike Fletcher, she did not hold their leftism against them.

Jean Starr Untermeyer's deep familiarity with Lowell allows her to correct many ridiculous stories that pictured the sheepdogs, for example, as a wild pack that frightened visitors:

> As I remember them—ranged in a circle at a respectful distance from the diningroom table, or guzzling their food from gray enamel pans at the hearth in the library—they suggested caricatures of nodding English judges in dirty wigs, rather than ferocious animals.

The stories about the terrorizing pets are, I suspect, the product of those who neither love nor have much knowledge of dogs and were upset at the very *idea* of so many animals in their vicinity.

Like Sergeant, Untermeyer notes all the minute particulars a la Boswell that make Lowell come to life. Thus we learn that Lowell had a footstool, "a small folding contrivance" that she carried with her everywhere. And she was always late for dinner even as she profusely apologized and vowed to do better the next time.

Jean was present when Lowell, visiting the Untermeyers and their guests in their New York City apartment, called herself the "last of the barons," openly admitting she slept with a revolver handy to shoot the intruders who would come to rob her of Sevenels and her wealthy privileges. The Untermeyers, after all, were not that far removed from the world of John Reed, the *New Masses*, and a generation of radicals that agitated against the capitalist colossus. Lowell could get really worked up over this threat to her position: "I had seen the dangerous red mount into Amy's usually controlled and alert face," Untermeyer recalled, "and I heard that strange note in her voice. I feared an apoplectic seizure."

Untermeyer did what only a true friend could do for Lowell. Jean rose, took Amy's hand, and led her into Jean's bedroom. "She came with me, docile as a child," Untermeyer reports. As soon as Lowell regained her composure, the two women rejoined the other guests, and, changing the subject, Lowell could "charm a bird off a bush."

Lowell's hysterical outburst made quite an impression on the Untermeyers who were discussing it when Amy returned to retrieve the footstool she had forgotten. The ensuing scene exposes an Amy Lowell who rarely appears in other accounts:

> It [the footstool] was quickly found and handed to her, but still she lingered. Ada was waiting downstairs in the cab. Louis and I stood with her in the hall. She looked at us brightly but uncertainly. "Louis, I'm sure, will forgive me," she said, "but I'm afraid Jean is angry with me. Will you forgive me, Jean?" "It's not a question of forgiving," I answered her. "Ignorant people give way to their prejudices, and times like these are bad. It's up to people like ourselves to hold the balance. When such a person as you goes off the deep end," I told her, "I'm really disturbed."

An agitated Amy got Jean to agree that they would meet the next day at Amy's hotel, although Jean was determined not to "talked over to her point of view." Amy left them that night with an anecdote that signaled, in Lowell's view, a coming age of barbarism. "You'd feel as I do if a German officer had pushed you right off the pavement. That's what happened to me." Untermeyer does not say anymore, but presumably this incident occurred in London at the outbreak of World War I. Rather than being sobered by Amy's parting "Parthian shot," however, the Untermeyers were amused at the picture of the "unequal contest" between Lowell and the German officer. And yet, later Jean took Amy's comment as a "lightening flash of intuition of the threat implicit in the tendencies already revealing themselves" in the nascent movements of fascism and communism.

Untermeyer concludes her memoir with an account of a visit she made to Ada Russell after Lowell's death. As Ada was reflecting on her own life, she regretted that Amy "could not look back as we were doing and realize how much had been wrested from fate." And this is where Elizabeth Shepley Sergeant and Jean Starr Untermeyer converge: in a profound understanding of just what a victory Lowell had made of her life:

> Yes, it was a brave life! We spoke of gain as well as loss. Sometimes in sorrow the horizon broadens: the personal takes its place in a larger scheme of values. We deplored that with Amy's going went also a quality not now so often cultivated or extolled: an old fashioned quality. They called it valor.

VIII

One reason why the figure of Amy Lowell caused a certain consternation is because it did not fit certain ingrained cultural conceptions. Curiously, few memoirists have acknowledged that their reactions to her had as much to do with what they thought a New England poet should look like as with the person before them. Margaret Widdemer, remembering her response to Lowell when Widdemer was a young aspiring writer, is an exception. Working for book collector, A. S. W. Rosenbach, Widdemer answered a query from Lowell about certain Keats and Shelley items the poet wanted to examine. "I remember the picture of her that the name made in my mind," Widdemer wrote: "A gentle spinster, slender, controlled, her pretty graying hair knotted low, dreaming over an old lover and the romantic poets in a gray gown longer than the fashion, straying in an old garden." In short, a relic.

A year later at a Poetry Society meeting in New York City, Widdemer got an eyeful of the real thing: "short, extremely stout, erect, and completely self-certain." Then came the inevitable wisecrack: "Her gown was a maroon cloth, so tight-fitting that somebody behind us whispered she looked like a sofa."

Unlike many who have commented on Lowell's figure, Widdemer did not merely note its impact on others but instead tried to fathom what being fat meant to Lowell. Like others, Widdemer noted the poet's "clear-cut features, delicately made small hands and feet, a good carriage, force and dignity"—all of which presumably mitigated an otherwise "grotesque" appearance. Widdemer had heard that at sixteen, Lowell had suffered a serious illness that had "left her with a glandular condition" that made it impossible for her to control her weight. In other words, Amy Lowell's story became that of a "small slender graceful girl," a young princess suddenly thrust into a corpulent shape. How cruel for a proud personality like Lowell's, Widdemer surmised. How much crueler yet that Lowell could do nothing about the ridicule and realize that people would make fun of her for something she could not help.

Hence Lowell, in Widdemer's view, fashioned an exquisite sense of what beauty was even as she developed a defiant, dominating, and even revengeful spirit. This craving for the esthetic helped Lowell bear the burden of her physical deformity. Or as Widdemer speculated: "Adoring beauty, with a poet's sensitiveness, I suppose Amy never forgot what she looked like." This may be so, but like so many who have commented on Lowell the person, Widdemer than recklessly links her reading of Lowell's psychological makeup to a poem, "En garde, messieurs," that is not even by Lowell in order to suggest that the poet became implacable in her quest to give "no quarter" to her critics.

This combative Lowell is manifested in her highly competitive and sometimes vindictive treatment of her fellow poets. Somehow, Lowell's grief and shame over her obesity accounts, Widdemer implies, for the kind of log-rolling Lowell engaged by puffing the work of others and expecting them to puff hers in return and in her resenting anyone who deviated from this corrupt bargaining among poets.

But Lowell's behavior is hardly unique in the fierce rivalries of literary life. It is an extraordinary stretch, to say the least, to see Lowell's campaigning for her kind of poet and that of her friends as some kind of pathology. The etiology of literary feuds and friendships simply cannot be reduced to this kind of psychologizing. That Lowell had been awful to Vachel Lindsey, withdrawing support for a tour of his because Lowell had heard reports that he had trashed her, is certainly to be deplored. But Lowell's bad behavior is hardly the result of a sensitivity over her surplus poundage, which, in Widdemer's imagination, colored everything Amy did. Widdemer's point is eviscerated anyway when she admits that Lindsay "joked a little roughly about everyone," and that a reporter probably exaggerated Lindsay's words when he was questioned about Amy's cigar smoking and other habits.. But surely Lowell could have expected more circumspection from a fellow poet who was relying on her help and surely understood how easy it was to make Lowell look ridiculous. In Widdemer's memoir, the story becomes a fable about poor Lindsay, not the badly used Lowell.

It get worse for Widdemer when she supposes:

> The psychotherapists have a phrase about "beckoning to you the thing you hate or dread." If you expect something unpleasant, they say, you unconsciously so act as to make it happen. I do think Amy beckoned the jeers to her, threw herself open, unnecessarily, to the ridicule—whether, unconsciously, that she might be punished for it, or a little, too, because it was terrific publicity. Or both.

Or both! Lowell was flamboyant, no doubt. But no more so than, say, Oscar Wilde. It is just as likely that Lowell decided *not* to brood on her obesity and *not* to sulk in private but rather to carry on in public as any other self-promoting writer might. On occasion, when her extravagantly proportioned figure became a public spectacle (as in that taxi ride with Fletcher) she did carry on, perhaps even enjoying herself, as Fletcher supposed.

Widdemer's account of the famous bathtub poem—as it came to be called—which Lowell read to a titillated Poetry Society of America audience that laughed at the vision of Lowell frolicking in her bath, does not seem an exercise in self-punishment so much as Lowell's unwillingness to defer to that organization's sense of propriety. She just read on without any concession to the rude snickers or any desire, apparently, to retaliate. It was enough for Amy Lowell to have her say, it seems. It is Widdemer's supposition, not Lowell's, that Lowell had expected too much of her audience, believing they would not associate her personally with what she was reading. Was Lowell not to read such a poem because of the way she looked?

If anything, Lowell's apparent aplomb could well be a sign of how well-adjusted she had become in the peace she made with her own imposing presence.

Revenge is such an overmastering theme in Widdemer's memoir that Amy Lowell emerges as almost a kind of allegorical figure, RETRIBUTION. Residents of the MacDowell colony, a refuge for writers, accepted an invitation to Sevenels, situated nearby, with "alacrity mingled with apprehension," Widdemer claimed. Not that Amy was not "great lady" and excellent host, serving elegant and delicious dinners accompanied with good talk. "But I think she rather liked to scare people at first, just a little," Widdemer feels obliged to add. Lowell might have replied: "Depends on the people."

Widdemer was one of the easily scared, she admitted. As a Lowell, Amy treated her guests, Widdemer supposed, like "interesting animals going through tricks for her." Or was this detached amusement a "defense mechanism"? Widdemer's uncertainty reflects, she implied, her own wariness and timidity, since she could not deny that Lowell was "brilliantly courteous" to her guests.

Widdemer is interesting on Lowell's dogs that were allowed into the library after dinner: "as completely poised and arrogantly agreeable as Amy herself could have been." It is a pleasure to learn their names from Widdemer, who was introduced to each one: Pamela and Joseph Andrews, Mr. Lovelace, Charles Grandison, Sophia Western, Tom Jones, Harriet Byron, or was it Clementina—Widdemer could not remember for sure. Guests received large damask napkins to protect their clothing from the wet muzzles of dogs drinking out of their water bowls. Widdemer saw that only dog lovers could be perfectly comfortable with this arrangement, although whether the present company liked dogs was never the topic of discussion. Eventually the dogs would exit and conversation continued. They performed real work, Widdemer insisted, roaming the grounds and fending off intruders.

Lowell had a gift for finding exactly the right subjects to draw out her guests. Gracing every party was Ada Russell, whose lovely speaking voice and gentle charm enchanted Widdemer. Amy had been "greatly pleased with Margaret," Russell assured Widdemer: "Most people think they have to talk to her about nothing but poets." Widdemer confessed that the compliment made her feel as though she was walking on air on her way home.

Widdemer concludes her memoir with an account of what Lowell told her about the contretemps with Ezra Pound, a story that culminates in Widdemer's view of the revengeful Amy. In Lowell's version it was Pound who came looking for her: "I met him in London. He wrote and asked if he could call. He enclosed an abjectly admiring letter about himself from May Sinclair." So, in Amy's words, she "let him come."

According to Widdemer, Pound had been used to intimidating Harriet Monroe, even boasting that he had made her his slave so that she published whatever he recommended. Lowell, in Widdemer's account, had to suffer Pound's extreme rudeness. Right then, Lowell decided, she told Widdemer, that would get the best of this insolent oaf:

> "I said nothing. That is," she added, "aloud. But what I said to myself was, 'This young man takes me for one more literary spinster, to be bullied into thrilled subjection by male brutality. All right, young man, I won't tell you what *I* think of *you*. But when I'm through with you, *your* Imagist movement is going to be *my* Imagist movement!' And," she ended, it was!"

Who knows if this reconstructed dialogue is accurate? If it is near the mark, then Lowell was indulging in some revisionism, collapsing her evolving notion of how to involve herself in the Imagist movement into a single epiphany. Perhaps she did already glimpse how she would outmaneuver Pound, although he was surely not so thuggish on their first meeting since he was, after all, seeking her support and other accounts suggest that he flattered Lowell.

To Widdemer, Lowell's story reflects her need for revenge. But the story falls flat, leading to no satisfactory conclusion in a memoir that ends by lamely calling Lowell an "unforgettable personality."

I like best what John Drinkwater said about Lowell at the Keats House meeting memorializing her—that she had "opportunities of being herself, of being sincere, that are not really given to many." Lowell sought and secured the freedom to be herself—still a rare and precious prize that few human beings have been able to attain.

7

Brief Portraits
Cameos
Walk-Ons

Somewhere within that face and form so closely resembling Holbein's Henry VIII was hidden a heart that the world and the critics missed.—Ferris Greenslet, *Under the Bridge: An Autobiography* (1943)

Handicapped as Amy had been from youth with a serious glandular malady, which made her form huge and disproportionate, she still moved with grace. Her hands and feet were quite beautiful. Amy's head was small and well proportioned. When dressed, she wore a false braid of hair like a tiara, in an effort to keep her head in balance with her body.—Eleanor Robson Belmont, *The Fabric of Memory* (1957)

Large of body, though not tall, wealthy, a patrician, she was snobbish to those who claimed social equality on any other basis than their talents. . . . Invalid in body, often moving with difficulty, I have seen her sitting at home like a chained eagle, lunging at what she called the pedantries of Harvard, of which her brother was president, or crushing with one claw some reviewer who lacked scholarship and a gentleman's education. A great human being, somewhat childish in her likes and dislikes, but immensely vital, she stirred all of us into activity, poets and critics alike.—Henry Seidel Canby, *American Memoir* (1947)

Amy Lowell towers above most contemporary versifiers like a sort of nineteenth century Savonarola, exhorting them to beware the pitfalls of sin and the ways of the devil. She is the sternest of Puritans; but over her gray sense of duty she wears a multitude of jewels. She wreathes herself in flowers, exotic colors flame from her hair, and while she consigns lust to the bonfire she makes sure that both lust and the bonfire are attractively tricked out with pretty words. Probably no great woman ever so successfully concealed herself by elaborate trappings. The poetical Miss Lowell reminds me occasionally of a whole-hearted and beautiful dowager who, afraid that her own person will fail to charm, hedges herself about with silks and satins, perfumes, flowers, jewels, and clanking metals, until she seems a veritable museum of *objets d'art*, and the real woman beneath, fine and true as she is, becomes discernible only to those who are patient enough to look and to wait The genius of Miss Lowell is based on a conflict—it is the quarrel of New England conservatism with an almost pagan love of the beautiful—and the result is, naturally enough, a firm code of denial, of duty in the strictest sense.

Miss Lowell's own life has been fulfilled by the most rigorous discipline. Ever since she undertook to write poetry, she has made its creation its entertainment, and its criticism her entire existence. She spends at least half her days in one of the most beautiful private libraries in the world—her own. Her life is organized for literature and is arranged to meet the demands made of it by the instinct to create! She understands *life* thoroughly; but she is afraid of it. She has spent her whole poetical career in disciplining her emotions. It is her mind only that wanders far afield. ---John Farrar, ed., *The Literary Spotlight* (1924)

When the war came, Amy was a little alarmed at the idea she might not be able to get home. Reassured on that point, she became the patriot anxious to help her fellow-countrymen, who were crowding into England from the war areas in considerable panic; and she pestered the American Ambassador for something to do. That ruthless humorist made her meet every train arriving from the Continent with a large notice hung from her neck: "American Citizens Apply Here. Amy was extremely sensitive about her abnormal size, and it must have been agony for her to display herself in this way. But she had pluck, and went through with it to the end.—Richard Aldington, *Life for Life's Sake: A Book of Reminiscences* (1941)

I was staying with Harold Laski . . . then at the height of his amazing youthful vitality, and eager to introduce me to the most interesting people in Cambridge. . . . I managed to create a sufficiently favorable impression [in a talk at the Harvard Union], though I gave the audience an uncompromising demonstration of my point of view. That no opposition became evident may have been due to the presiding presence of Miss Amy Lowell, who was mainly responsible for my being there at all. Although by no means in agreement with my opinions, she was a generous admirer of my work, and had written to tell me that I was the one man whom the Harvard undergraduates wanted to hear. After the meeting we spent a memorable evening in her beautiful library. Listening to her and [Harold] Laski, I felt almost non-existent as a talker. They were a remarkably contrasted couple—he, small, boyishly brilliant, provocative in argument, and essentially generous and idealistic; she, stout and masculine, jocularly downright and dogmatic, smoking a long Manila cigar, and completely confident that "Imagism" was the poetry of the future.—Siegfried Sassoon, *Siegfried's Journey 1916-1920* (1946).

January 1917, Poetry Society of America event in New York City:

Wildrid Wilson Gibson was guest of honor and began his speech by saying that he was somewhat at a loss here in America where he found our poets divided into schools, as he was not an "ist" and followed no "ism."

This was enough for Amy, and when her turn came she let loose the vials, not of her wrath but of her wit, declaring he was the most hopelessly ingrained "ist," as he was a *realist*. Getting excited, she kept the diners in a round of mirth, punctuating her remarks by tossing up a gold-mesh vanity bag and catching it, with each new sally. In all public lectures Miss Lowell spoke from manuscript, but on intimate occasions she threw this aside and was one of the wittiest and most brilliant of speakers.—Jessie B. Rittenhouse, *My House of Life: An Autobiography* (1934)

At one annual dinner of the Poetry Society she rose—after arriving late and causing half a dozen of us at the speaker's table to move—and said rudely when called upon, "I had expected to speak of humor here to-night but as anything less humorous than the remarks of the speaker who has just sat down is inconceivable, I will speak of something else."—Cale Younger Rice, *Bridging the Years* (1939)

Amy Lowell came to Chicago while I was secretary and woman of all work at the Little Theatre, and I was delegated to look after her during her visit because she was lecturing under our exclusive aegis. She and I got along like mortise and tenon after the first few minutes of shyness on my part and, on hers, the natural art of a Lowell from the land of the cod, where as the doggerel has it, certain families, the Lowells included, "speak only to God." She settled back in the biggest chair we could find, took out one of her famous big black cigars, lighted it, and explained to me what the whole new movement in poetry was about. The cigar was a little disconcerting because I had never seen a woman smoke a cigar (her favorites were Corona Coronas), and it seemed a bit *outré* for the sister of the president of Harvard and a sprig of the sedate Lowell family tree.—Fanny Butcher, *Many Lives—One Love* (1972)

Amy Lowell, of course, came to Chicago to see what was going on and to prevent anything going wrong. But Harriet Monroe handled her with tact, and for my part, I think she gave her more commendation than she deserved. . . . Amy Lowell's descent upon Chicago was comparable to that of an Italian diva . . . I rather shrank from meeting her; but Harriet Monroe said that it would be discourteous if I did not pay my compliments to her by calling. So I went to her suite in the Congress Hotel, where she was enthroned in a state attended by a companion-secretary. She offered me a Corona cigar, and smoke two of these huge rollers of nicotine while I smoked one. We talked very pleasantly until I made some comment on a literary judgment that she had recently published; whereupon she stuck up her finger with authority and exclaimed, "Your reasons, sir?" Not wishing to get into a debate with her I glided away from the invited dialectic. But all the while I was fascinated with her eyes. They were large and blue and luminous. I have never seen more beautiful eyes, or eyes that bespoke the light that was back of them with more effulgent power.—Edgar Lee Masters, *Across Spoon River* (1936)

Amy Lowell came and went amid the same sort of furor as last year, with a brave air of a Cyrano de Bergerac facing life's impulchritudes. . ."—Carl Sandburg to Alice Corbin

Henderson, September 16, 1916. *The Letters of Carl Sandburg* (1968)

[T]here was sturdy obstreperous Amy Lowell breathing for revolt as the mares of Diomedes breathed fire . . . .

The stage of the theatre, which was tiny, had been set with a formal arrangement of flats and curtains, and a chair placed for Miss Lowell, with a reading lamp beside it. But someone had miscalculated, and the space through which she was to enter was too small. She made an attempt to get in sidewise, but stuck. I was petrified, and the audience snickered. When the setting had been pushed apart Amy entered, wearing one of the most absurd little hats ever perpetrated, and sat her great bulk down in the chair. But at once she got up again and demanded that the chair and the lamp be moved. A nervous young man appeared and jiggered with them for a long time, only at last to satisfy Amy by putting them back within an inch of where they had at first stood. It was a difficult beginning, but such was the force of the woman that in a very few minutes all this was forgotten, and the reading was an immense success.

Once, several years later, I had a set-to with one of her famous black cigars. We had gone with her, after a lecture, to her room at a hotel, and she offered me a cigar—somewhat maliciously, I thought. I was not to be daunted, and accepted. Presently, when the weed was about half gone, I began to feel very strange. . . . Amy suddenly ordered food, and so reprieved me for the time being. I put the half-burned cigar out of sight behind my coffee cup and afterwards, though I was very much better, I lit a cigarette. Anyone else would have let me get by with it, but not Amy. She learned around, looking for the evidence, and said gleefully, "Aha! You could not finish it!" And I could only acknowledge myself beaten.

Once, after she and I had had a literary tiff in one of the magazines—I no longer remember what it was about—the next time I saw her she came down a long roomful of people with outstretched hands, beaming cordially and booming out, "Here comes my best enemy!" There was no bearing malice against anyone as dynamic as Amy, no matter what she did; but I could never find her *simpatico*, and perhaps others felt as I did, because I was told she longed for love but could seldom find it.—Eunice Tietjens, *The World at My Shoulder* (1938)

Miss Amy Lowell came to the shop often. Her autograph, seen in our guest-book, is precise and elegant. She was kind in heart and liberal in her purchases of books as befitted a great collector. No dealer had cause to find fault with her in either of these respects, yet if he were sensitive the half-hour of her call might be a questionable pleasure, for she had a sharp tongue. The directness of her expression left no doubt as to what her views were on any point under discussion, and her dominating spirit was likely to beat down the opposition to a cause which she might espouse.

I saw her at a dinner given in her honor on the eve of her intended sailing for London in the spring of 1925. It was a pleasant party not untempered in the minds of some by forebodings, for she was not in good health. There was a large company gathered in the ballroom of the Somerset. As a dozen speakers offered their tribute of appreciation, eulogy, essay, or impromptu remark from the orchid-adorned table, Miss Lowell smilingly sipped coffee and smoked the inevitable cigar. When the speaking was finished she read two poems, receiving an offering of flowers in a silver bowl, bowed, and the affair was over. I wonder how many of those present sensed the shortness of her hold on life or realized that this meeting with her was the last.—Charles E. Goodspeed, *Yankee Bookseller* (1937)

I'm not so sure of him [Edwin Arlington Robinson]. Nor damn it all, of Monstrous Mistress Amy!—Conrad Aiken to John Gould Fletcher [April 1917]

I saw that my old enemy was dead, Amy, noble Amy. . . . I was surprisingly moved and saddened, and still am. A damned shame. . . . A lot of color will go out of American letters with Amy; for all her vanities and faults a magnificent creature.—Conrad Aiken to Robert N. Linscott, May 14, 1925—*Selected Letters of Conrad Aiken* (1978)

One evening in May 1925—it doesn't seem so long ago—a paralytic stroke defeated the most dynamic personality in modern American poetry: Amy Lowell. Somehow, something more than her own warfare came to an end. I felt at the time that the whole spirit of controversy had closed. The battles she fought with others, the battles we were led into against our own will, were over. Those of us who had never missed her before missed her for the first time. Those for whom she fought their own battles missed her most; they were her intimates in life and poetry. Though I knew Amy Lowell over a period of about ten years, saw and corresponded with her sporadically, I did not learn to know her at all well until the final year. I begin with this personal note because it colors my present perspective. I was never a deep admirer of her work until her latest poems appeared. Before that time, I felt that she echoed, in her abundant versatility, every other poet but herself. She was a brilliant mocking bird of other styles. There was no mood, no character, no form she could not achieve on the surface; in her amazing vitality, she played every conceivable role. Her own role was not the role of an artist, so much as a mummer's—an actress in male attire. One thought of her as a buccaneer scuttling the craft of conservatives and even going so far as to strip radical vessels of their best prizes. But the masculine Miss Lowell was more than a pirate. The one time I dined at the Brookline estate, I felt as if I were in audience with a later Roman emperor—possibly Nero fiddling among the flames. And yet, I learned to know her a little more closely, perhaps more accurately. In unguarded moments, she seemed an immensely feminine person, not without innocence and wistfulness, and I decided—if one can ever decide anything—that her abnormal ambition and industry had obscured her true character. The role she played for the world was masculine, valiant, combative—and the inner being, private, lonely, susceptible to human fragility.—Alfred Kreymborg, *One Singing Strength: An Outline of American Poetry* (1929)

Endnotes

[1] For this volume, I have decided not to write about Lowell's friendships with women—other than in my chapter, "Remembering Amy Lowell." In my forthcoming biography of Lowell, however, I plan to extensively explore Lowell's friendships with writers such as H. D. and Bryher—neither of whom, alas, wrote memoirs of Lowell. But fortunately there is an extensive record of correspondence between Lowell and H. D. and Lowell and Bryher in Lowell's papers at Houghton Library, Harvard University.

[2] Louis Untermeyer, *The Letters of Robert Frost to Louis Untermeyer*. New York: Holt, Rinehart and Winston, 1963. "Clement Wood, a renegade Southerner, had come to New York from Birmingham, Alabama, where, after succeeding Justice Hugo Black as presiding magistrate of the Central Recorder's Court, he had been removed for "lack of judicial temperament." . . . He was twenty-six, three years younger than myself, when I met him in 1914, and we became close friends. I liked his unflagging buoyancy and admired his insurgent spirit." Wood wrote song lyrics, poetry, and hackwork biographies.

³ Russell actively cooperated with Damon in the writing of Lowell's biography. But she left no written record of her relationship with Lowell and destroyed Lowell's letters to her at Lowell's request. Damon is reticent about the private lives of Lowell and Russell. Jean Gould is the only biographer that has come close to supposing the two women were lovers. It is hardly speculative to say, however, that their travels together—not to mention the household they shared—invited gossip about their liaison.

⁴ Vorticism has been a difficult movement to define. For Pound, it represented the next stage of Imagism, which he wanted to relate to the other arts, especially painting and sculpture. Lowell would have rejected the term because it was allied with cubism and other efforts to dislocate realism by using flat, bold colors and geometrical shapes. Art became a vortex, an all-encompassing, engulfing experience. This form of abstract art was antithetical to Lowell's precise observing eye. Most commentators have implied Lowell was confused and nettled by Pound's switch to Vorticism. For example, Barbara Guest, *Herself Defined: The Poet H. D. and Her World* (New York: Doubleday, 1984, pp. 67-68) treats Lowell as a naïf expecting Pound & Co. to provide her with "an Imagist welcome [dinner] in her honor" on her second trip to London. When Pound and his allies prove recalcitrant, Lowell, with her "thick skin" shrugs them off. Guest quotes from Pound's Canto LXXVII, referring to Lowell during this period as a "telluric mass"—that is, a kind of immense body, a continent of flesh that could not be budged from her place. But it is more likely that she understood him quite well and rejected an art that divorced itself from the look of objects as they actually exist in space. Pound's tyrannical promotion of Vorticism is of a piece with fascist tendencies that would also have put off Lowell. In his biography of John Gould Fletcher, Ben F. Johnson III notes: "Vorticism

also contained Modernism's incipient social ideology: an anti-democratic skepticism, a readiness to advocate violence, and a distaste for rational humanism. One of the ten propositions contained in the first *BLAST* [the Vorticist journal] boasted: "We are Primitive Mercenaries in the Modern World." Amy Lowell's basic conservatism was affronted by the deliberate crudeness of the journal, Johnson suggests. Conservatism, perhaps, but also an affronted democratic spirit.

[5] I deal more extensively with Fletcher's view of Pound and Lowell, and of Fletcher's own friendship with Lowell, in a separate chapter.

[6] I find this still to be true in the case of recent selections of her poetry published by the Library of America and Rutgers University Press. Both books seek to represent the range of Lowell's poetry rather than establishing a canon of her finest work.

[7] Writers were always commenting on how he looked and sounded. Healey, p. 450, quotes Wyndham Lewis's description of a "flabby lemon and pink giant, who hung his mouth open as though he were an animal at the zoo inviting buns—especially when ladies were present. Over the gaping mouth damply depended the ragged ends of a pale lemon moustache . . ."

[8] See Carl Rollyson, *Rebecca West: A Modern Sibyl* (New York: iUniverse, 2009), p. 33.

[9] If I speak rather confidently of how Russell would have reacted to discussion of Ford's piece, it is because I have examined a draft of Damon's biography in his papers at Brown University Library and noted that Russell requested that he excise several mentions of Lowell's obesity.

[10] Quoted in Adam Piette, "'The Garden' as Modernist Imitation: Samain, Lowell, H. D."

[11] "Amy Lowell Visits London," *The New England Quarterly* 46 (September 1973): 442.

[12] Both letters are quoted in Healey, p. 444.

[13] Diana Trilling, ed., *The Selected Letters of D. H. Lawrence* (New York: Farrar, Straus and Cudahy, 1958), p. 79.

[14] Witter Byner, *Journey with Genius: Recollections and Reflections Concerning the D. H. Lawrences* (New York: The John Day Company, 1951), p 145.

[15] See Byner, p. xiii.

[16] Byner, p. 145, suggests that Lawrence would have regarded Lowell's sending him money as not "an unnatural gratuity. He was himself always ready to hand over a sizable part of his own small balance, when he had one, to almost any friend in need, with no thought of gratitude or even repayment."

[17] The only reading of the Lowell/Frost relationship that comes close to mine is by Frost's granddaughter, Lesley Lee Francis, "A Decade of "Stirring Times": Robert Frost and Amy Lowell," *The New England Quarterly* 59 (December 1986): 508-22.

[18] Included in Harley Farnsworth MacNair, *Florence Ayscough and Amy Lowell: Correspondence of a Friendship* (Chicago: University of Chicago Press, 1945).

[19] One of the "Hundred Views of Fuji" by Hokusai, first published in *Poetry* 1917 and reprinted in *Amy Lowell: Selected Poems*, edited by Melissa Bradshaw and Adrienne Munich (New Brunswick: Rutgers University Press 2004).

Sanahide Kodama, *American Poetry and Japanese Culture* (Hamden, CT: Archon Books, 1984), p. 30, mentions Sandburg's familiarity with Hokusai. Kodama also helps illuminate Lowell's Hokusai poem, noting that Lowell owned a book, *One Hundred Views of Fuji* that contained a picture of "a man sitting and holding a small cup, in which is reflected Mount Fuji dancing like a dropped leaf."

[20] Jean Catel, reviewing the Lowell/Ayscough letters, *Modern Philology* 44 (November 1946): 132-33.

[21] *New England Quarterly* 19 (September 1946): 398-403.

[22] Richard LeGallienne, "A Caravan From China Comes," *The New York Times Book Review*, January 15, 1922, p. 41.

[23] "Humanity Made Accessible," *The New York Times Book Review*, May 26, 1957, p. 4.

[24] See Francis A. Johns, "Arthur Waley and Amy Lowell: A Note," *The Journal of the Rutgers University Libraries* 44 (1): 17-22.

[25] William Leonard Schwartz, "A Study of Amy Lowell's Far Eastern Verse," *Modern Language Notes* 43 (March 1928): 145-52.

[26] This perceptive essay is included in *Amy Lowell, American Modern*, edited by Adrienne Munich and Melissa Bradshaw (New Brunswick, NJ: Rutgers University Press, 2004).

[27] So does Adrienne Munich in her introduction to *Amy Lowell: American Modern*. She deems Lowell's Chinese poems "powerfully beautiful translations."

[28] This poem is reprinted in *Amy Lowell: Selected Poems*, edited by Honor Moore (Library of America, 2004).

[29] Pound's version of Li Po is available in *Personae: Collected Short Poems of Ezra Pound* (New York: New Directions, 1971).

[30] Shortly after writing these words, I obtained a copy of Yunge Huang's *Transpacific Displacement: Intertextual Travel in Twentieth-Century American Literature* (2002), a fitting companion to Yoshihara's work. Huang argues that Ayscough and Lowell created a modern poetics just as important as Pound's work with Ernest Fenollosa, although the latter pair, Huang notes, "has always been adulated as a superior comparison by the biased (most gender-biased) critics." He attributes to Ayscough and Lowell a new mode of conceptualizing Asia." Whereas Pound uses Fenollosa's translations as grist for his modernist poetry, Lowell's more prosy poems constitute, in Huang's words, a travelogue—a deliberate journey through a culture. Lowell's effects are cumulative, and she eschews the intensification of the line that distinguishes Pound's Imagism. As Huang concludes, "Lowell seemed very concerned with particular characters, with those tourist spots in Chinese poetry that attract intertextual travelers like herself and Ayscough. Not understanding or having no patience with Lowell's methods, critics have been unable to grasp the beauty of Lowell's lines

[31] Included in *Can Grande's Castle* (1918).

[32] *Fierce Solitude: A Life of John Gould Fletcher* (Fayetteville: University of Arkansas Press, 1994), pp. 57-58.

[33] Johnson, p. 58.

[34] Lowell's memory of this meeting dovetails with Fletcher's. See *Tendencies in Modern American Poetry*, p. 290.

[35] All quotations are from Leighton Rudolph, Lucas Carpenter, and Ethel C. Simpson, ed., *Selected Letters of John Gould Fletcher* (Fayetteville: University of Arkansas Press, 1996.

[36] Quoted in Johnson, 103.

[37] Johnson, p. 92.

[38] Sassoon, p. 182.

[39] To Daisy Fletcher, 17 January [1916]

[40] To Conrad Aiken, 22 October 1918.

[41] The record of the memorial for Lowell at Keats House is at the London Metropolitan Archives.

[42] Fletcher's review is reprinted in Lucas Carpenter, ed., *Selected Essays of John Gould Fletcher* (Fayetteville: The University Press of Arkansas, 1989.

[43] Damon, p. 622.

[44] *Under the Bridge: An Autobiography* (1943).

Appendix A

Imagists

By the end of the nineteenth century, poets in Britain and in America were seeking a new, modern way to write verse. In Britain, the reigning movements in poetry and the arts---Romanticism and Victorianism—seem to have run their course. Romantic lyric poetry as exemplified by Percy Bysshe Shelley (1792-1822) and John Keats (1795-1821), for example, had degenerated (many poets believed) into self-indulgence, so that poets seemed so preoccupied with their own subjectivity that the greater world was largely ignored. The result was a poetry that was precious and clichéd. In other words, poets relied on stock words and phrases such as "thee" and "thou" and "the orb of heaven" that tended to remove poetry from reality, from the day-to-day experience of most people. Poets were, in effect, just repeating what other poets had to say. And Victorian poets had made matters worse, by writing with sentimentality and decorum, thus eschewing the raw, robust radicalism that poets of Byron's generation cultivated.

In the United States, poetry as an art was in a kind of limbo. The two greatest American poets of the nineteenth century—Walt Whitman (1891-1892) and Emily Dickinson (1830-1886)—had largely been ignored by their contemporaries and these full extent of the contributions to American poetry were discounted in the 1880's and 1890's by what came to be termed the "genteel tradition," one that like the Victorians used poetry to express acceptable sentiments and avoided outspoken experiments with poetry. Dickinson and Whitman would not receive their due until the 1920s, after a new generation of writers and critics rediscovered them, seeing in their work the seeds of a bold, new, modern poetry.

Of course these broad generalizations should not obscure the significant works of poets such as Alfred Tennyson (1809-1892) and Robert Browning (1812-1892) or of the nascent poetry of writers like Stephen Crane (1871-1900), a writer who died while still quite young just as he was experimenting with verse that anticipated Imagism. But the state of Anglo-American poetry at the end of the nineteenth century seemed moribund to a new generation that would begin to be published in the first two decades of the twentieth century.

The key figure involved in the development of new experimental forms of poetry, including Imagism, was the American poet and critic Ezra Pound (1885-1972). Finding few sources of encouragement in his native land, Pound settled in London, quickly befriending older, established poets like W. B. Yeats (1865-1939) who seemed eager to write a sharper, grittier, kind of verse that would distinguish them from their nineteenth century predecessors and contemporaries.

Ezra Pound and the advent of Imagism

Pound used London as his poetry laboratory. He quickly made friends with promising young writers such as Richard Aldington (1892-1962), H. D. (Hilda Doolittle, 1886-1961), John Gould Fletcher (1886-1950), and F. S. Flint (1885-1960)—all of whom would become part of the Imagist movement. Pound also met a British philosopher, T. E. Hulme (1883-1917), who believed in the revival of classicism, which emphasized not the personality of the writer but the form of the work. The structure of works of art ought to be the poet's concern in an age of science, Hulme argued, and not the poet's feelings per se.

From his talks with Hulme Pound formulated the cardinal principles of Imagism: direct treatment of subject matter (in practice, this would mean an almost photographic portrayal of objects and scenes) and elimination of any word or phrase that did not absolutely contribute to the presentation of the poem. Other tenets of Imagism as Pound expounded them were mainly technical advice to poets—to write in musical phrases rather than in rigid meter. Pound was certainly not opposed to traditional forms of poetry such as the sonnet, but the emphasis of his program led to experiments with so-called free verse—lines that did not have end rhymes and that could be of varying lengths and numbers of syllables.

Pound was also one of the first Anglo-American poets to experiment with translations of Japanese poetry in order to introduce into Western verse the terse, image-dominated lines of *hokku*: "As cool as the pale wet leaves/ of lily-of-the-valley/ She lay beside me in the dawn." The epigrammatic style served as an antidote to the elaborate and turgid excesses of Romantic and Victorian poetry. Built around a single simile this short poem, entitled "Alba," functioned as an astringent, ridding the poet's style of any unnecessary word or expression.

Pound inaugurated the Imagist movement with an anthology *Des Imagistes*, published in March 1914. As fiercely as Pound believed in the new poetry, he did little to advance his cause by introducing or campaigning for the work of the writers he had included in *Des Imagistes*. His fellow poets in Britain and America were galvanized by his efforts, but they made little headway in attracting readers or in persuading reviewers and publishers that Imagism was a significant departure from past practice that deserved broader attention and approval.

Pound's influence was exerted mainly through journals in England and in America, especially in *Poetry*, a magazine established by Chicago poet and editor Harriet Monroe (1860-1936) in 1912. It was in that magazine that Amy Lowell

(1874-1925), just beginning her career as a poet, read Pound's strictures about poetry and the requirements of Imagism. She regarded his work as a call to scrap her own rather traditional verse and begin anew. Her enthusiasm over Pound's pieces in *Poetry* were to fundamentally impact the history of poetry in America and abroad in ways Pound had not envisioned, especially in her ability to make poetry itself a public event that would entice a growing and avid audience not only for Imagism but for work of many other modern poets.

Amy Lowell, Imagism, and Amygism

Lowell, the descendant of a prominent New England family, famous for its achievements in both business and the arts, published her first book of poetry, *A Dome of Many-Coloured Glass*, in 1912. She had been meditating a career as a poet for nearly a decade, although even as a child she wrote poetry and beginning in her twenties lectured in Boston on literary subjects. The title of her first book, taken from Shelley's famous poem, "Adonais" mourning the death of John Keats, reflected Lowell's love of Romantic literature and her adherence to traditional forms of poetry. But her first volume excited little interest among reviewers and won her a very small audience. The disappointed Lowell, perusing the pages of Harriet Monroe's *Poetry* became excited by Pound's extolling of Imagism. Virtually at once Lowell decided to jettison the writing of conventional poetry, and in the spring of 1913 she set out for London, the site, she later explained in *Tendencies in American Poetry* (1917), of the most exciting developments in modern verse.

In London, Lowell met with Pound, who introduced her to his Imagist colleagues: Richard Aldington, H. D., F. S. Flint, and John Gould Fletcher. Lowell would also meet other remarkable writers in Pound's circle as well as D. H. Lawrence (1885-1930), with whom she would correspond to the end of her life. Lowell quickly ascertained that many of these poets resented Pound's highhanded methods. They were also dismayed that their new poetry had so little impact on Anglo-American readers. To Pound's outrage, Lowell set about corralling this disaffected group, promising to put them into print in America, and in general furthering the Imagist cause. She had both the promotional know-how and the financial resources to make her a creditable alternative to Pound.

Lowell lacked only bona fides as an Imagist poet herself. Industrious and an avid learner, she was producing Imagist poems before she returned to the United States in the fall of 1913. By 1915, Lowell had produced the first of three Imagist anthologies, featuring her work and that of Aldington , H.D., Flint, Lawrence, and Fletcher. Pound excluded himself, deeply resenting Lowell's takeover of a movement he believed belonged to him.

The work of these six poets in the Imagist anthologies is broadly representative of the modern poetry that Pound was promulgating. But Lowell, a keen publicist, made sure that her three volumes contained prefaces that set out the Imagist program, thus linking the efforts of individual poets to a grand vision of the way modern poetry, especially in free verse, was making literary history. Unlike Pound, Lowell made no effort to dictate to her colleagues. Thus each Imagist anthology was composed of poems that each poet deemed worthy of inclusion. Pound scorned this democratic, Imagist confederation, calling it "Amygism," by which he meant not only to criticize Lowell's outsize ego but also to express his disapproval of what he deemed her crass popularizing of poetry, which, in his view, diluted the power and ultimately the quality of the poems presented as examples of Imagism.

As the Imagist anthologies demonstrate, however, the poetry was of exceptional quality. Of course, not every poem met Pound's highest standards, but to Lowell that seemed less important than her efforts to make poetry a vital part of Anglo-American life. Not only did she want to energize contemporary poetry, she also wanted it to grow in numbers of readers and institutions that could support the careers of poets and make poetry itself count for more in the lives of her fellow Americans.

A consideration of the individual poets who published in the Imagist anthologies provides the best way to comprehend the experiments, achievements, and ambitions of the Imagist movement.

Richard Aldington

The youngest of the Imagist poets, Aldington sought a way back to the Greeks. He admired the austerity of Greek art and as an Imagist he sought to write unadorned verse, the opposite of the opulent, flowing lines associated with Victorian poets like Tennyson. Similarly, Aldington wanted to avoid the self-referential qualities of Romantic poetry, in which the poet becomes the hero of his own work.

Some of Aldington's best poetry was the result of his service in World War I. He brought to his description of that war a stark, brutal, and precise power of observation. That Imagists eschewed open expression of their feelings did not mean, however, that the poetry could not be intense and the product of personal emotion and experience. Here, for example, are lines from "Soliloquy-I" describing the horrors of war: "Dead men should be so still, austere, / And beautiful, / Not wobbling carrion roped upon a cart . . . "

Aldington's avidity for Greek art is suggested in his desire to see the dead in repose like figures in classical sculpture. The full shock of war is reflected in choosing the word "carrion," the word for the rotting flesh of animals, including human beings. Although the poet is disgusted with this scene of horror, he does not, in fact, make his aversion explicit, allowing, in true

Imagist fashion, the wording of the understated line to carry the weight of his emotions.

The poet wishes to aesthetize the world, to make it beautiful, Aldington implies. But the reality of war thwarts the aesthete's purposes. A true Imagist, the poet presents the indelible image of a body tied to a moving vehicle. This is no refined tableau of war, but war in all its immediacy and grim fatality.

Like other Imagists, Aldington wrote in free verse; that is, he did not use end rhymes or lines of equal length. Thus "And beautiful" is given its own line, with no attempt to provide an even, balanced rhythm. On the contrary, the poem stops and starts in lines of uneven length—in this case in order to emphasize the abruptness of war not to mention the staccato nature of his thoughts in this horrid, shifting panorama of gore. The poet's tone is clipped, and he is, so to speak, short with himself and upset that war so overturns his aestheticism, his desire for what dead men "should" look like. War, in other words, is presented as an affront to the poet, a breakup in the pattern of life and art as he would wish to experience it. A reluctant witness to war, the Imagist poet must nevertheless record what he sees, and in recording what he sees, allow his emotions and perceptions to inhere in his choice of words without forcing the scene to conform to the sentiments he wishes to express.

H. D.

Born in Bethlehem, Pennsylvania, Hilda Doolittle befriended Ezra Pound when he was attending the University of Pennsylvania in Philadelphia. Later they renewed their acquaintance in 1911 when she arrived in London. It was Pound who persuaded her to sign herself "H. D. Imagiste," and when she married Richard Aldington, the circle of Imagists became all that tighter. And yet H. D., like Aldington, was willing to break with Pound over the promotion of Imagism, lending her genius to all three of Amy Lowell's Imagist anthologies.

Glenn Hughes has called H. D. the perfect Imagist—a judgment many critics have ratified. She exemplified the movement in short, terse poems such as "Oread," a densely metaphorical six-line poem that begins, "Whirl up, sea— / whirl your pointed pines." Repetition, or what Lowell liked to call "return" is evident in the poet's use of whirl to evoke the jagged swirls of the sea, seen in the poem as a kind of pine forest swaying—an exact, quite literal picture. Pines do often come to a point and they create a sort of wave effect in heavy winds. In other words, the metaphorical and literal tend to merge in H. D.'s spare, austere verse, which derives, in part, from her sharing Aldington's admiration for the unadorned style of classical poetry.

Critics have sometimes expressed reservations about H. D.'s poetry of isolated images, finding it cold, if vivid, and they are hard put to find a meaning in her literal/metaphorical poems. But like Lowell, who was also accused of writing without passion, H. D. believed that her Imagism was full of emotion brought to bear on a world that readers ought to be able to observe objectively in her poems. In "Oread," moreover, the poet does exhibit her own feelings in lines such as "hurl your green over us." This address to the sea, in other words, is about not only the poet's but humanity's intense attraction to the immensity and power of nature, to the basic elements (water and land) of life. This is hardly, in other words, a poem that is simply devoted to description.

John Gould Fletcher

Of all the Imagists at work in London, Fletcher had the most profound and immediate impact on Amy Lowell. Her conversation with him not only led to a major change in her style but also to her conviction that Fletcher and his colleagues deserved a larger audience than Pound was capable of attracting.

Coming to distrust an increasing erratic Ezra Pound, Fletcher shared his poems with Lowell, who saw in them a rhythm, diction, and pattern that represented a decisive break with her nineteenth-century models. An excited Lowell would write about London and New York attempting to capture the urban rhythms of Fletcher's book, *Irradiations*, which she secured a publisher for. Thus his poem about a rainstorm in the city captures the movement and scene of modern life in lines such as, "Sudden scurry of umbrellas: / Bending, recurved blossoms of the storm." Here Fletcher exemplifies an Imagism that is more fanciful than H. D.'s and yet still anchored in an actual moment. The literal becomes metaphorical swiftly and economically with the umbrellas taking the shape of a kind of flower show, fashioned out of the poet's observation of people opening their umbrellas. The mass movements of people make it look as though the umbrellas have a life of their own like flowers bowed and reshaped by rain.

F. S. Flint

The least well known of the Imagists, Flint, a poet and critic, served the movement best in several highly regarded critical essays. Only a few of his poems survive as excellent examples of Imagism, for he tended too often toward padding his lines to suit certain rhythms to the detriment of the overall force and coherence of his work. His poetry seems too much like one of his favorites, John Keats—that is, Flint favors the romantic lyric far more than the hard-edged images of H. D., for example. Thus in his poem, "London," he rejects the daylight images of a pale green sky and birds hopping on a lawn and prefers to think of his beautiful city by moonlight: "among the stars,/ I think of her / and the glow her passing/

sheds on men." While the images seem pedestrian, the lines do reflect the Imagist concentration on the value of short lines that segregate images in order to enhance their maximum impact. His rhythms too are refreshing, far more relaxed than the intensity of Romantic lyrics, and without a rigid rhyme scheme he achieves a natural cadence that suited the Imagist's notion of what modern poetry should look like.

D. H. Lawrence

A fine poet and novelist, Lawrence never really considered himself an Imagist, but Lowell, realizing Lawrence was a great artist, persuaded him to join the movement, and he was grateful for her efforts in promoting his work. To Lowell, Lawrence also deserved inclusion in her anthologies because certain of his poems did conform to the Imagist credo. Indeed, in a letter to him she quoted an example of his Imagism: "The morning breaks like a pomegranate/ In a shining crack of red." Lawrence brought incredible energy to Imagism, a dynamism Lowell saw reflected in these lines which crackle with the kind of exuberance and explosiveness that was Imagism at its boldest and best.

Amy Lowell

Although Lowell, like H. D., has been called an unemotional poet—a writer content to simply report what she observed was Robert Frost's verdict on her work—in fact she brought an erotic intensity to Imagism: "You are an almond flower unsheathed/ Leaping and flickering between budded branches," she writes in "White and Green." Fletcher's influence is felt in her effort to capture the movement and shapes of nature as an index of her own passionate mood. The budded branches suggest the bursting and blossoming of love without Lowell's ever making her feelings the focus of her lines.

A good deal of Lowell's finest Imagist poems are set in gardens (she had a beautiful garden and estate in Brookline, Massachusetts) that become metaphors for her exploration of a remarkable range of subjects. Her masterpiece, "Patterns," for example, written in 1917, evokes in the setting of Flanders both the wars of the 17th century and World War I but also the life of a woman caught in the pattern a woman of her time is supposed to follow as well as in the pattern of war that takes her beloved away from her.

The End of Imagism

Lowell felt that by 1920, after the publication of three Imagist anthologies, the work of Imagism per se had been accomplished. In other words, the principles and practices of the Imagist poet had become a part of modern poetry and the need for a separate movement no longer seemed urgent or even necessary. H. D. and the other Imagists would continue to write poems that exemplified the movement, but these poets ranged far from a strict adherence to the program Pound initially established—as did Pound himself.

No account of modern poetry can ignore the pervasive influence of Imagism while at the same time acknowledging that the movement had limited aims and in the end had to supercede itself by having it poets engage in producing other examples of modern poetry.

Sources for further study

Aldington, Richard. *Life for Life's Sake.* New York: Viking, 1941). Chapter IX discusses Aldington's involvement with the Imagists.

Fletcher, John Gould. *Life is My Song.* New York: Rinehart & Winston, 1937. Describes his relationship with Lowell, the development of his Imagist poetry and its influence on her work.

Hughes, Glenn. *Imagism and the Imagists: A Study in Modern Poetry.* Stanford: Stanford University Press, 1924. Still one of the standard studies, Hughes interviewed the Imagists and wrote separate chapters on the movement and on individual Imagist poets. His work is a deft combination of literary history, literary criticism, and biography. His bibliography includes many contemporary reactions to Imagism.

Jones, Peter, ed. *Imagist Poetry.* New York: Penguin, 2002. Contains an informative introduction as well as selections from T. E. Hulme's influential Imagist poems, the work of the major Imagist poets but also of others writing in the Imagist tradition such as William Carlos Williams and Marianne Moore.

Lowell, Amy. *Tendencies in Modern American Poetry.* Boston: Houghton-Mifflin, 1917. Includes a long, perceptive chapter on H. D. and John Gould Fletcher by the leader of the Imagist movement.

Pratt, William, ed. *The Imagist Poem.* Story Line Press, 2001. A revision and expansion of a work first published in 1963. Includes an informative introduction and bibliography, selections from the work of major Imagist poets as well as work by major poets such as T. E. Eliot and Carl Sandburg who were influenced by the Imagist movement.

Appendix B

Amy Lowell: Selected Poetry

Absence
The Onlooker
Before the Altar
A Fairy Tale
The Starling
The Green Bowl
In A Garden
Astigmatism
Bath
The Dinner Party
A Tulip Garden
An Aquarium
Guns as Keys
A Decade
Venus Transiens
The Precinct, Rochester
The Cyclists
The Captured Goddess
The Shadow
Madonna of the Evening Flowers
White and Green
Patterns

Absence

My cup is empty to-night,
Cold and dry are its sides,
Chilled by the wind from the open window.
Empty and void, it sparkles white in the moonlight.
The room is filled with the strange scent
Of wistaria blossoms.
They sway in the moon's radiance
And tap against the wall.
But the cup of my heart is still,
And cold, and empty.

When you come, it brims
Red and trembling with blood,
Heart's blood for your drinking;
To fill your mouth with love
And the bitter-sweet taste of a soul.

The On-Looker

Suppose I plant you
Like wide-eyed Helen
On the battlements
Of weary Troy,
Clutching the parapet with desperate hands.
She, too, gazes at a battlefield
Where bright vermillion plumes and metal whiteness
Shock and sparkle and go down with groans.
Her glances strike the rocking battle.
Again—again—
Recoiling from it
Like baffed spear-heads fallen from a brazen shield.
The ancients at her elbow counsel patience
and contingencies;
Such to a woman stretched upon a bed of battle.
Who bargained for this only in the whispering arras
Enclosed about a midnight of enchantment.

Before the Altar

Before the Altar, bowed, he stands
With empty hands;
Upon it perfumed offerings burn
Wreathing with smoke the sacrificial urn.
Not one of all these has he given,
No flame of his has leapt to Heaven
Firesouled, vermilion-hearted,
Forked, and darted,
Consuming what a few spare pence
Have cheaply bought, to fling from hence
In idly-asked petition.
His sole condition
Love and poverty.
And while the moon
Swings slow across the sky,
Athwart a waving pine tree,
And soon
Tips all the needles there
With silver sparkles, bitterly
He gazes, while his soul
Grows hard with thinking of the poorness of his dole.

"Shining and distant Goddess, hear my prayer
Where you swim in the high air!
With charity look down on me,
Under this tree,
Tending the gifts I have not brought,
The rare and goodly things
I have not sought.
Instead, take from me all my life!

"Upon the wings
Of shimmering moonbeams

I pack my poet's dreams
For you.
My wearying strife,
My courage, my loss,
Into the night I toss
For you.
Golden Divinity,
Deign to look down on me
Who so unworthily
Offers to you:
All life has known,
Seeds withered unsown,
Hopes turning quick to fears,
Laughter which dies in tears.
The shredded remnant of a man
Is all the span
And compass of my offering to you.

"Empty and silent, I
Kneel before your pure, calm majesty.
On this stone, in this urn
I pour my heart and watch it burn,
Myself the sacrifice; but be
Still unmoved: Divinity."
From the altar, bathed in moonlight,
The smoke rose straight in the quiet night.

A Fairy Tale

On winter nights beside the nursery fire
We read the fairy tale, while glowing coals
Builded its pictures. There before our eyes
We saw the vaulted hall of traceried stone
Uprear itself, the distant ceiling hung
With pendent stalactites like frozen vines;
And all along the walls at intervals,
Curled upwards into pillars, roses climbed,
And ramped and were confined, and clustered leaves
Divided where there peered a laughing face.
The foliage seemed to rustle in the wind,
A silent murmur, carved in still, gray stone.
High pointed windows pierced the southern wall
Whence proud escutcheons flung prismatic fires
To stain the tessellated marble floor
With pools of red, and quivering green, and blue;
And in the shade beyond the further door,
Its sober squares of black and white were hid
Beneath a restless, shuffling, wide-eyed mob
Of lackeys and retainers come to view
The Christening.
A sudden blare of trumpets, and the throng
About the entrance parted as the guests
Filed singly in with rare and precious gifts.
Our eager fancies noted all they brought,
The glorious, unattainable delights!
But always there was one unbidden guest
Who cursed the child and left it bitterness.

The fire falls asunder, all is changed,
I am no more a child, and what I see
Is not a fairy tale, but life, my life.
The gifts are there, the many pleasant things:

Health, wealth, long-settled friendships, with a name
Which honors all who bear it, and the power
Of making words obedient. This is much;
But overshadowing all is still the curse,
That never shall I be fulfilled by love!
Along the parching highroad of the world
No other soul shall bear mine company.
Always shall I be teased with semblances,
With cruel impostures, which I trust awhile
Then dash to pieces, as a careless boy
Flings a kaleidoscope, which shattering
Strews all the ground about with coloured sherds.
So I behold my visions on the ground
No longer radiant, an ignoble heap
Of broken, dusty glass. And so, unlit,
Even by hope or faith, my dragging steps
Force me forever through the passing days.

The Starling

"'I can't get out', said the starling."
Sterne's `Sentimental Journey'.

Forever the impenetrable wall
Of self confines my poor rebellious soul,
I never see the towering white clouds roll
Before a sturdy wind, save through the small
Barred window of my jail. I live a thrall
With all my outer life a clipped, square hole,
Rectangular; a fraction of a scroll
Unwound and winding like a worsted ball.
My thoughts are grown uneager and depressed
Through being always mine, my fancy's wings
Are moulted and the feathers blown away.
I weary for desires never guessed,
For alien passions, strange imaginings,
To be some other person for a day.

The Green Bowl

This little bowl is like a mossy pool
In a Spring wood, where dogtooth violets grow
Nodding in chequered sunshine of the trees;
A quiet place, still, with the sound of birds,
Where, though unseen, is heard the endless song
And murmur of the never resting sea.
'T was winter, Roger, when you made this cup,
But coming Spring guided your eager hand
And round the edge you fashioned young green leaves,
A proper chalice made to hold the shy
And little flowers of the woods. And here
They will forget their sad uprooting, lost
In pleasure that this circle of bright leaves
Should be their setting; once more they will dream
They hear winds wandering through lofty trees
And see the sun smiling between the leaves.

In a Garden

Gushing from the mouths of stone men
To spread at ease under the sky
In granite-lipped basins,
Where iris dabble their feet
And rustle to a passing wind,
The water fills the garden with its rushing,
In the midst of the quiet of close-clipped lawns.

Damp smell the ferns in tunnels of stone,
Where trickle and plash the fountains,
Marble fountains, yellowed with much water.

Splashing down moss-tarnished steps
It falls, the water;
And the air is throbbing with it.
With its gurgling and running.
With its leaping, and deep, cool murmur.

And I wished for night and you.
I wanted to see you in the swimming-pool,
White and shining in the silver-flecked water.
While the moon rode over the garden,
High in the arch of night,
And the scent of the lilacs was heavy with stillness.

Night, and the water, and you in your whiteness, bathing!

Astigmatism

To Ezra Pound: with Much Friendship and Admiration and Some Differences of Opinion

The Poet took his walking-stick
Of fine and polished ebony.
Set in the close-grained wood
Were quaint devices;
Patterns in ambers,
And in the clouded green of jades.
The top was smooth, yellow ivory,
And a tassel of tarnished gold
Hung by a faded cord from a hole
Pierced in the hard wood,
Circled with silver.
For years the Poet had wrought upon this cane.
His wealth had gone to enrich it,
His experiences to pattern it,
His labour to fashion and burnish it.
To him it was perfect,
A work of art and a weapon,
A delight and a defence.
The Poet took his walking-stick
And walked abroad.

Peace be with you, Brother.

The Poet came to a meadow.
Sifted through the grass were daisies,
Open-mouthed, wondering, they gazed at the sun.
The Poet struck them with his cane.
The little heads flew off, and they lay
Dying, open-mouthed and wondering,
On the hard ground.

"They are useless. They are not roses," said the Poet.

Peace be with you, Brother. Go your ways.

The Poet came to a stream.
Purple and blue flags waded in the water;
In among them hopped the speckled frogs;
The wind slid through them, rustling.
The Poet lifted his cane,
And the iris heads fell into the water.
They floated away, torn and drowning.
"Wretched flowers," said the Poet,
"They are not roses."

Peace be with you, Brother. It is your affair.

The Poet came to a garden.
Dahlias ripened against a wall,
Gillyflowers stood up bravely for all their short stature,
And a trumpet-vine covered an arbour
With the red and gold of its blossoms.
Red and gold like the brass notes of trumpets.
The Poet knocked off the stiff heads of the dahlias,
And his cane lopped the gillyflowers at the ground.
Then he severed the trumpet-blossoms from their stems.
Red and gold they lay scattered,
Red and gold, as on a battle field;
Red and gold, prone and dying.
"They were not roses," said the Poet.
Peace be with you, Brother.
But behind you is destruction, and waste places.

The Poet came home at evening,
And in the candle-light
He wiped and polished his cane.

The orange candle flame leaped in the yellow ambers,
And made the jades undulate like green pools.
It played along the bright ebony,
And glowed in the top of cream-coloured ivory.
But these things were dead,
Only the candle-light made them seem to move.
"It is a pity there were no roses," said the Poet.

Peace be with you, Brother. You have chosen your part.

Bath

The day is fresh-washed and fair, and there is a smell of tulips and narcissus in the air.

The sunshine pours in at the bath-room window and bores through the water in the bath-tub in lathes and planes of greenish-white. It cleaves the water into flaws like a jewel, and cracks it to bright light.

Little spots of sunshine lie on the surface of the water and dance, dance, and their reflections wobble deliciously over the ceiling; a stir of my finger sets them whirring, reeling. I move a foot, and the planes of light in the water jar. I lie back and laugh, and let the green-white water, the sun-flawed beryl water, flow over me. The day is almost too bright to bear, the green water covers me from the too bright day. I will lie here awhile and play with the water and the sun spots.

The sky is blue and high. A crow flaps by the window, and there is a whiff of tulips and narcissus in the air.

The Dinner Party

So . . . they said,
With their wine glasses delicately poised
Mocking at the thing they cannot understand
So . . . they said again
Amused and insolent.
The silver on the table glittered,
And the red wine in the glasses
Seemed the blood I had wasted
In a foolish cause.

A Tulip Garden

Guarded within the old red wall's embrace,
Marshalled like soldiers in gay company,
The tulips stand arrayed.
Here infantry
Wheels out into the sunlight.
What bold grace
Sets off their tunics, white with crimson lace!
Here are platoons of gold-frocked cavalry,
With scarlet sabres tossing in the eye
Of purple batteries, every gun in place.
Forward they come, with flaunting colours spread,
With torches burning, stepping out in time
To some quick, unheard march.
Our ears are dead,
We cannot catch the tune.
In pantomime
Parades that army.
With our utmost powers
We hear the wind stream through a bed of flowers.

An Aquarium

Streaks of green and yellow iridescence,
Silver shiftings,
Rings veering out of rings,
Silver -- gold --
Grey-green opaqueness sliding down,
With sharp white bubbles
Shooting and dancing,
Flinging quickly outward.
Nosing the bubbles,
Swallowing them,
Fish.
Blue shadows against silver-saffron water,
The light rippling over them
In steel-bright tremors.
Outspread translucent fins
Flute, fold, and relapse;
The threaded light prints through them on the pebbles
In scarcely tarnished twinklings.
Curving of spotted spines,
Slow up-shifts,
Lazy convolutions:
Then a sudden swift straightening
And darting below:
Oblique grey shadows
Athwart a pale casement.
Roped and curled,
Green man-eating eels
Slumber in undulate rhythms,
With crests laid horizontal on their backs.
Barred fish,
Striped fish,
Uneven disks of fish,
Slip, slide, whirl, turn,

And never touch.
Metallic blue fish,
With fins wide and yellow and swaying
Like Oriental fans,
Hold the sun in their bellies
And glow with light:
Blue brilliance cut by black bars.
An oblong pane of straw-coloured shimmer,
Across it, in a tangent,
A smear of rose, black, silver.
Short twists and upstartings,
Rose-black, in a setting of bubbles:
Sunshine playing between red and black flowers
On a blue and gold lawn.
Shadows and polished surfaces,
Facets of mauve and purple,
A constant modulation of values.
Shaft-shaped,
With green bead eyes;
Thick-nosed,
Heliotrope-coloured;
Swift spots of chrysolite and coral;
In the midst of green, pearl, amethyst irradiations.

Outside,
A willow-tree flickers
With little white jerks,
And long blue waves
Rise steadily beyond the outer islands.

The Thatched House Unroofed by an Autumn Gale

IT is the Eighth Month, the very height of Autumn.
The wind rages and roars.
It tears off three layers of my grass-roof.
The thatch flies – it crosses the river – it is scattered about in the open spaces by the river.
High-flying, it hangs, tangled and floating, from the tops of forest trees;
Low-flying, it whirls – turns – and sinks into the hollows of the marsh.
The swarm of small boys from the South Village laugh at me because I am old and feeble.
How dare they act like thieves and robbers before my face,
Openly seizing my thatch and running into my bamboo grove?
My lips are scorched, my mouth dry, I scream at them, but to no purpose.
I return, leaning on my staff. I sigh and breathe heavily.

Presently, of a sudden, the wind ceases. The clouds are the colour of ink.
The Autumn sky is endless – endless – stretching toward dusk and night.

CH'ANG KAN

BY LI T'AI-PO

WHEN the hair of your Unworthy One first began to cover her forehead,
She picked flowers and played in front of the door.
Then you, my Lover, came riding a bamboo horse.
We ran round and round the bed, and tossed about the sweetmeats of green plums.
We both lived in the village of Ch'ang Kan.
We were both very young, and knew neither jealousy nor suspicion.
At fourteen, I became the wife of my Lord.
I could not yet lay aside my face of shame;
I hung my head, facing the dark wall;
You might call me a thousand times, not once would I turn round.
At fifteen, I stopped frowning.
I wanted to be with you, as dust with its ashes.
I often thought that you were the faithful man who clung to the bridge-post,
That I should never be obliged to ascend to the Looking-for-Husband Ledge.
When I was sixteen, my Lord went far away,
To the Ch'ü T'ang Chasm and the Whirling Water Rock of the Yü River

From **"Guns as Keys: And The Great Gate Swings"**

At Mishima in the Province of Kai,
Three men are trying to measure a pine tree
By the length of their outstretched arms.
Trying to span the bole of a huge pine tree
By the spread of their lifted arms.
Attempting to compress its girth
Within the limit of their extended arms.
Beyond, Fuji, Majestic, inevitable,
Wreathed over by wisps of cloud.
The clouds draw about the mountain,
But there are gaps.
The men reach about the pine tree,
But their hands break apart;
The rough bark escapes their hand clasps;
The tree is unencircled.
Three men are trying to measure the stem of a gigantic pine
    tree,
With their arms,
At Mishima in the Province of Kai.

* * *

The road is hilly
Outside the Tiger Gate,
And striped with shadows from the bow moon
Slowly sinking on the horizon.
The roadway twinkles with the bobbing of paper lanterns,
Melon-shaped, round, oblong,
Lighting the steps of those who pass along it;
And there is a sweet singing of many semi,
From the cages which an insect-seller
Carries on his back.

* * *

Nigi-oi of Matsuba-ya
Celebrated oiran,
Courtesan of unrivalled beauty,
The great silk mercer, Mitsui,
Counts himself a fortunate man
As he watches her parade in front of him
In her robes of glazed blue silk
Embroidered with singing nightingales.
He puffs his little silver pipe
And arranges a fold of her dress.
He parts it at the neck
And laughs when the falling plum-blossoms
Tickle her naked breasts.
The next morning he makes out a bill
To the Director of the Dutch Factory at Nagasaki
For three times the amount of the goods
Forwarded that day in two small junks
In the care of a trusted clerk.

* * *

The one hundred and sixty streets in the Sanno quarter
Are honey-gold, Honey-gold from the gold-foil screens in the
     houses,
Honey-gold from the fresh yellow mats;
The lintels are draped with bright colours,
And from eaves and poles
Red and white paper lanterns
Glitter and swing.
Through the one hundred and sixty decorated streets of the
     Sanno quarter,
Trails the procession,
With a bright slowness,

The music of flutes and drums.
Great white sails of cotton
Belly out along the honey-gold streets.
Sword bearers, Spear bearers, Mask bearers,
Grinning masks of mountain genii,
And a white cock on a drum
Above a purple sheet.
Over the flower hats of the people,
Shines the sacred palanquin,
"Car of gentle motion,"
Upheld by fifty men,
Stalwart servants of the god.
Bending under the weight of mirror-black lacquer,
Of pillars and roof-tree Wrapped in chased and gilded copper.
Portly silk tassels sway to the marching of feet,
Wreaths of gold and silver flowers
Shoot sudden scintillations at the gold-foil screens.
The golden phoenix on the roof of the palanquin
Spreads it wings,
And seems about to take flight
Over the one hundred and sixty streets
Straight into the white heart
Of the curved blue sky. Six black oxen,
With white and red trappings,
Draw platforms on which are musicians, dancers, actors,
Who posture and sing,
Dance and parade,
Up and down the honey-gold streets,
To the sweet playing of flutes,
And the ever-repeating beat of heavy drums,
To the constant banging of heavily beaten drums.
To the insistent repeating rhythm of beautiful great drums.

* * *

The ladies,
Wistaria Blossom, Cloth-of-Silk, and Deep Snow,
With their ten attendants,
Are come to Asakusa
To gaze at peonies.
To admire crimson-carmine peonies,
To stare in admiration at bomb-shaped, white and sulphur
    peonies,
To caress with a soft finger
Single, rose-flat peonies,
Tight, incurved, red-edged peonies,
Spin-wheel circle, amaranth peonies.
To smell the acrid pungeance of peony blooms,
And dream for months afterwards
Of the temple garden at Asakusa,
Where they walked together
Looking at peonies.

* * *

A Daimyo's procession
Winds between to green hills,
A line of thin, sharp, shining, pointed spears
Above red coats
And yellow mushroom hats.
A man leading an ox
Has cast himself upon the ground,
He rubs his forehead in the dust,
While his ox gazes with wide, moon eyes
At the glittering spears
Majestically parading
Between two green hills.

* * *

Tiger rain on the temple bridge of carved green-stone,
Slanting tiger lines of rain on the lichened lanterns of the gateway,
On the stone statues of mythical warriors.
Striped rain making the bells of the pagoda roofs flutter,
Tiger-footing on the bluish stones of the court-yard,
Beating, snapping, on the cheese-rounds of open umbrellas,
Licking, tiger-tongued, over the straw mat which a pilgrim wears upon his shoulders,
Gnawing, tiger-toothed, into the paper mask
Which he carries on his back.
Tiger-clawed rain scattering the peach-blossoms,
Tiger tails of rain lashing furiously among the cryptomerias.

* * *

The beautiful dresses,
Blue, Green, Mauve, Yellow;
And the beautiful green pointed hats
Like Chinese porcelains!
See, a band of geisha
Is imitating the state procession of a Corean Ambassador,
Under painted streamers,
On an early afternoon.

* * *

Down the ninety-mile rapids
Of the Heaven Dragon River,
He came,
With his bowmen,
And his spearmen,
Borne in a gilded palanquin,
To pass the Winter in Yedo
By the Shôgun's decree.

To pass the Winter idling in the Yoshiwara,
While his bowmen and spearmen
Gamble away their rusted weapons
Every evening
At the Hour of the Cock.

* * *

Outside the drapery shop of Taketani Sabai,
Strips of dyed cloth are hanging out to dry.
Fine Arimitsu cloth,
Fine blue and white cloth,
Falling from a high staging,
Falling like falling water,
Like blue and white unbroken water
Sliding over a high cliff,
Like the Ono Fall on the Kisokaido Road.
Outside the shop of Taketani Sabai,
They have hung the fine dyed cloth
In strips out to dry.

* * *

On the floor of the reception room of the Palace
They have laid a white quilt,
And on the quilt, two red rugs;
And they have set up two screens of white paper
To hide that which should not be seen.
At the four corners, they have placed lanterns,
And now they come,
Six attendants,
Three to sit on either side of the condemned man,
Walking slowly.
Three to the right,
Three to the left,

And he between them
In his dress of ceremony
With the great wings.
Shadow wings, thrown by the lantern light,
Trail over the red rugs to the polished floor,
Trail away unnoticed,
For there is a sharp glitter from a dagger
Borne past the lanterns on a silver tray.
"O my Master, I would borrow your sword,
For it may be a consolation to you
To perish by a sword to which you are accustomed."
Stone, the face of the condemned man,
Stone, the face of the executioner,
And yet before this moment
These were master and pupil,
Honoured and according homage,
And this is an act of honourable devotion.
Each face is passive,
Hewed as out of strong stone,
Cold as a statue above a temple porch.
Down slips the dress of ceremony to the girdle.
Plunge the dagger to its hilt.
A trickle of blood runs along the white flesh
And soaks into the girdle silk.
Slowly across from left to right,
Slowly, upcutting at the end,
But the executioner leaps to his feet,
Poises the sword—
Did it flash, hover, descend?
There is a thud, a horrible rolling,
And the heavy sound of a loosened, falling body,
Then only the throbbing of blood
Spurting into the red rugs.
For he who was a man is that thing
Crumpled up on the floor,

Broken, and crushed into the red rugs.
The friend wipes the sword,
And his face is calm and frozen
As a stone statue on a Winter night
Above a temple gateway.

* * *

Postlude
In the castle moat, lotus flowers are blooming,
They shine with the light of an early moon
Brightening above the Castle towers.
They shine in the dark circles of their unreflecting leaves.
Pale blossoms,
Pale towers,
Pale moon,
Deserted ancient moat
About an ancient stronghold,
Your bowmen are departed,
Your strong walls are silent,
Their only echo
A croaking of frogs.
Frogs croaking at the moon
In the ancient moat
Of an ancient, crumbling Castle.

A Decade

When you came, you were like red wine and honey,
And the taste of you burnt my mouth with its sweetness.
Now you are like morning bread,
Smooth and pleasant.
I hardly taste you at all for I know your savour,
But I am completely nourished.

Venus Transiens

Tell me,
Was Venus more beautiful
Than you are,
When she topped
The crinkled waves,
Drifting shoreward
On her plaited shell?
Was Botticelli's vision
Fairer than mine;
And were the painted rosebuds
He tossed his lady
Of better worth
Than the words I blow about you
To cover your too great loveliness
As with a gauze
Of misted silver?

For me,
You stand poised
In the blue and bouyant air,
Cinctured by bright winds,
Treading the sunlight.
And the waves which precede you
Ripple and stir
The sands at my feet.

The Precinct, Rochester

The tall yellow hollyhocks stand,
Still and straight,
With their round blossoms spread open,
In the quiet sunshine.
And still is the old Roman wall,
Rough with jagged bits of flint,
And jutting stones,
Old and cragged,
Quite still in its antiquity.
The pear-trees press their branches against it,
And feeling it warm and kindly,
The little pears ripen to yellow and red.
They hang heavy, bursting with juice,
Against the wall.
So old, so still!
The sky is still.
The clouds make no sound
As they slide away
Beyond the Cathedral Tower,
To the river,
And the sea.
It is very quiet,
Very sunny.
The myrtle flowers stretch themselves in the sunshine,
But make no sound.
The roses push their little tendrils up,
And climb higher and higher.
In spots they have climbed over the wall.
But they are very still,
They do not seem to move.
And the old wall carries them
Without effort, and quietly
Ripens and shields the vines and blossoms.

A bird in a plane-tree
Sings a few notes,
Cadenced and perfect
They weave into the silence.
The Cathedral bell knocks,
One, two, three, and again,
And then again.
It is a quiet sound,
Calling to prayer,
Hardly scattering the stillness,
Only making it close in more densely.
The gardener picks ripe gooseberries
For the Dean's supper to-night.
It is very quiet,
Very regulated and mellow.
But the wall is old,
It has known many days.
It is a Roman wall,
Left-over and forgotten.
Beyond the Cathedral Close
Yelp and mutter the discontents of people not mellow,
Not well-regulated.
People who care more for bread than for beauty,
Who would break the tombs of saints,
And give the painted windows of churches
To their children for toys.
People who say: "They are dead, we live!
The world is for the living."
Fools! It is always the dead who breed.
Crush the ripe fruit, and cast it aside,
Yet its seeds shall fructify,
And trees rise where your huts were standing.
But the little people are ignorant,
They chaffer, and swarm.
They gnaw like rats,

And the foundations of the Cathedral are honeycombed.
The Dean is in the Chapter House;
He is reading the architect's bill
For the completed restoration of the Cathedral.
He will have ripe gooseberries for supper,
And then he will walk up and down the path
By the wall,
And admire the snapdragons and dahlias,
Thinking how quiet and peaceful
The garden is.
The old wall will watch him,
Very quietly and patiently it will watch.
For the wall is old,
It is a Roman wall.

The Cyclists

Spread on the roadway,
With open-blown jackets,
Like black, soaring pinions,
They swoop down the hillside,
The Cyclists.
Seeming dark-plumaged
Birds, after carrion,
Careening and circling,
Over the dying of England.
She lies with her bosom
Beneath them, no longer
The Dominant Mother,
The Virile—but rotting
Before time.
The smell of her, tainted,
Has bitten their nostrils.
Exultant they hover,
And shadow the sun with
Foreboding.

The Captured Goddess

Over the housetops,
Above the rotating chimney-pots,
I have seen a shiver of amethyst,
And blue and cinnamon have flickered
A moment,
At the far end of a dusty street.
Through sheeted rain
Has come a lustre of crimson,
And I have watched moonbeams
Hushed by a film of palest green.
It was her wings, Goddess!
Who stepped over the clouds,
And laid her rainbow feathers
Aslant on the currents of the air.
I followed her for long,
With gazing eyes and stumbling feet.
I cared not where she led me,
My eyes were full of colours:
Saffrons, rubies, the yellows of beryls,
And the indigo-blue of quartz;
Flights of rose, layers of chrysoprase,
Points of orange, spirals of vermilion,
The spotted gold of tiger-lily petals,
The loud pink of bursting hydrangeas.
I followed,
And watched for the flashing of her wings.
In the city I found her,
The narrow-streeted city.
In the market-place I came upon her,
Bound and trembling.
Her fluted wings were fastened to her sides with cords,
She was naked and cold,
For that day the wind blew

Without sunshine.
Men chaffered for her,
They bargained in silver and gold,
In copper, in wheat,
And called their bids across the market-place.
The Goddess wept.
Hiding my face I fled,
And the grey wind hissed behind me,
Along the narrow streets.

The Shadow

Paul Jannes was working very late,
For this watch must be done by eight
To-morrow or the Cardinal
Would certainly be vexed.
Of all His customers the old prelate
Was the most important, for his state
Descended to his watches and rings,
And he gave his mistresses many things
To make them forget his age and smile
When he paid visits, and they could while
The time away with a diamond locket
Exceedingly well.
So they picked his pocket,
And he paid in jewels for his slobbering kisses.
This watch was made to buy him blisses
From an Austrian countess on her way
Home, and she meant to start next day.
 Paul worked by the pointed, tulip-flame
Of a tallow candle, and became
So absorbed, that his old clock made him wince
Striking the hour a moment since.
Its echo, only half apprehended,
Lingered about the room. He ended
Screwing the little rubies in,
Setting the wheels to lock and spin,
Curling the infinitesimal springs,
Fixing the filigree hands. Chippings
Of precious stones lay strewn about.
The table before him was a rout
Of splashes and sparks of coloured light.
There was yellow gold in sheets, and quite
A heap of emeralds, and steel.
Here was a gem, there was a wheel.

And glasses lay like limpid lakes
Shining and still, and there were flakes
Of silver, and shavings of pearl,
And little wires all awhirl
With the light of the candle.
He took the watch
And wound its hands about to match
The time, then glanced up to take the hour
From the hanging clock.
Good, Merciful Power!
How came that shadow on the wall,
No woman was in the room! His tall
Chiffonier stood gaunt behind
His chair. His old cloak, rabbit-lined,
Hung from a peg. The door was closed.
Just for a moment he must have dozed.
He looked again, and saw it plain.
The silhouette made a blue-black stain
On the opposite wall, and it never wavered
Even when the candle quavered
Under his panting breath. What made
That beautiful, dreadful thing, that shade
Of something so lovely, so exquisite,
Cast from a substance which the sight
Had not been tutored to perceive?
Paul brushed his eyes across his sleeve.
Clear-cut, the Shadow on the wall
Gleamed black, and never moved at all.
 Paul's watches were like amulets,
Wrought into patterns and rosettes;
The cases were all set with stones,
And wreathing lines, and shining zones.
He knew the beauty in a curve,
And the Shadow tortured every nerve
With its perfect rhythm of outline

Cutting the whitewashed wall. So fine
Was the neck he knew he could have spanned
It about with the fingers of one hand.
The chin rose to a mouth he guessed,
But could not see, the lips were pressed
Loosely together, the edges close,
And the proud and delicate line of the nose
Melted into a brow, and there
Broke into undulant waves of hair.
The lady was edged with the stamp of race.
A singular vision in such a place.
 He moved the candle to the tall
Chiffonier; the Shadow stayed on the wall.
He threw his cloak upon a chair,
And still the lady's face was there.
From every corner of the room
He saw, in the patch of light, the gloom
That was the lady. Her violet bloom
Was almost brighter than that which came
From his candle's tulip-flame.
He set the filigree hands; he laid
The watch in the case which he had made;
He put on his rabbit cloak, and snuffed
His candle out. The room seemed stuffed
With darkness. Softly he crossed the floor,
And let himself out through the door.
 The sun was flashing from every pin
And wheel, when Paul let himself in.
The whitewashed walls were hot with light.
The room was the core of a chrysolite,
Burning and shimmering with fiery might.
The sun was so bright that no shadow could fall
From the furniture upon the wall.
Paul sighed as he looked at the empty space
Where a glare usurped the lady's place.

He settled himself to his work, but his mind
Wandered, and he would wake to find
His hand suspended, his eyes grown dim,
And nothing advanced beyond the rim
Of his dreaming. The Cardinal sent to pay
For his watch, which had purchased so fine a day.
But Paul could hardly touch the gold,
It seemed the price of his Shadow, sold.
With the first twilight he struck a match
And watched the little blue stars hatch
Into an egg of perfect flame.
He lit his candle, and almost in shame
At his eagerness, lifted his eyes.
The Shadow was there, and its precise
Outline etched the cold, white wall.
The young man swore, "By God! You, Paul,
There's something the matter with your brain.
Go home now and sleep off the strain."
 The next day was a storm, the rain
Whispered and scratched at the window-pane.
A grey and shadowless morning filled
The little shop. The watches, chilled,
Were dead and sparkless as burnt-out coals.
The gems lay on the table like shoals
Of stranded shells, their colours faded,
Mere heaps of stone, dull and degraded.
Paul's head was heavy, his hands obeyed
No orders, for his fancy strayed.
His work became a simple round
Of watches repaired and watches wound.
The slanting ribbons of the rain
Broke themselves on the window-pane,
But Paul saw the silver lines in vain.
Only when the candle was lit
And on the wall just opposite

He watched again the coming of IT,
Could he trace a line for the joy of his soul
And over his hands regain control.
 Paul lingered late in his shop that night
And the designs which his delight
Sketched on paper seemed to be
A tribute offered wistfully
To the beautiful shadow of her who came
And hovered over his candle flame.
In the morning he selected all
His perfect jacinths. One large opal
Hung like a milky, rainbow moon
In the centre, and blown in loose festoon
The red stones quivered on silver threads
To the outer edge, where a single, fine
Band of mother-of-pearl the line
Completed. On the other side,
The creamy porcelain of the face
Bore diamond hours, and no lace
Of cotton or silk could ever be
Tossed into being more airily
Than the filmy golden hands; the time
Seemed to tick away in rhyme.
When, at dusk, the Shadow grew
Upon the wall, Paul's work was through.
Holding the watch, he spoke to her:
"Lady, Beautiful Shadow, stir
Into one brief sign of being.
Turn your eyes this way, and seeing
This watch, made from those sweet curves
Where your hair from your forehead swerves,
Accept the gift which I have wrought
With your fairness in my thought.
Grant me this, and I shall be
Honoured overwhelmingly."

The Shadow rested black and still,
And the wind sighed over the window-sill.
 Paul put the despised watch away
And laid out before him his array
Of stones and metals, and when the morning
Struck the stones to their best adorning,
He chose the brightest, and this new watch
Was so light and thin it seemed to catch
The sunlight's nothingness, and its gleam.
Topazes ran in a foamy stream
Over the cover, the hands were studded
With garnets, and seemed red roses, budded.
The face was of crystal, and engraved
Upon it the figures flashed and waved
With zircons, and beryls, and amethysts.
It took a week to make, and his trysts
At night with the Shadow were his alone.
Paul swore not to speak till his task was done.
The night that the jewel was worthy to give.
Paul watched the long hours of daylight live
To the faintest streak; then lit his light,
And sharp against the wall's pure white
The outline of the Shadow started
Into form. His burning-hearted
Words so long imprisoned swelled
To tumbling speech.
Like one compelled,
He told the lady all his love,
And holding out the watch above
His head, he knelt, imploring some
Littlest sign.
The Shadow was dumb.
 Weeks passed, Paul worked in fevered haste,
And everything he made he placed
Before his lady. The Shadow kept

Its perfect passiveness. Paul wept.
He wooed her with the work of his hands,
He waited for those dear commands
She never gave. No word, no motion,
Eased the ache of his devotion.
His days passed in a strain of toil,
His nights burnt up in a seething coil.
Seasons shot by, uncognisant
He worked. The Shadow came to haunt
Even his days. Sometimes quite plain.
He saw on the wall the blackberry stain
Of his lady's picture. No sun was bright
Enough to dazzle that from his sight.
 There were moments when he groaned to see
His life spilled out so uselessly,
Begging for boons the Shade refused,
His finest workmanship abused,
The iridescent bubbles he blew
Into lovely existence, poor and few
In the shadowed eyes. Then he would curse
Himself and her! The Universe!
And more, the beauty he could not make,
And give her, for her comfort's sake!
He would beat his weary, empty hands
Upon the table, would hold up strands
Of silver and gold, and ask her why
She scorned the best which he could buy.
He would pray as to some high-niched saint,
That she would cure him of the taint
Of failure. He would clutch the wall
With his bleeding fingers, if she should fall
He could catch, and hold her, and make her live!
With sobs he would ask her to forgive
All he had done. And broken, spent,
He would call himself impertinent;

Presumptuous; a tradesman; a nothing; driven
To madness by the sight of Heaven.
At other times he would take the things
He had made, and winding them on strings,
Hang garlands before her, and burn perfumes,
Chanting strangely, while the fumes
Wreathed and blotted the shadow face,
As with a cloudy, nacreous lace.
There were days when he wooed as a lover, sighed
In tenderness, spoke to his bride,
Urged her to patience, said his skill
Should break the spell. A man's sworn will
Could compass life, even that, he knew.
By Christ's Blood! He would prove it true!
The edge of the Shadow never blurred.
The lips of the Shadow never stirred.
 He would climb on chairs to reach her lips,
And pat her hair with his finger-tips.
But instead of young, warm flesh returning
His warmth, the wall was cold and burning
Like stinging ice, and his passion, chilled,
Lay in his heart like some dead thing killed
At the moment of birth. Then, deadly sick,
He would lie in a swoon for hours, while thick
Phantasmagoria crowded his brain,
And his body shrieked in the clutch of pain.
The crisis passed, he would wake and smile
With a vacant joy, half-imbecile
And quite confused, not being certain
Why he was suffering; a curtain
Fallen over the tortured mind beguiled
His sorrow. Like a little child
He would play with his watches and gems, with glee
Calling the Shadow to look and see
How the spots on the ceiling danced prettily

When he flashed his stones. "Mother, the green
Has slid so cunningly in between
The blue and the yellow. Oh, please look down!"
Then, with a pitiful, puzzled frown,
He would get up slowly from his play
And walk round the room, feeling his way
From table to chair, from chair to door,
Stepping over the cracks in the floor,
Till reaching the table again, her face
Would bring recollection, and no solace
Could balm his hurt till unconsciousness
Stifled him and his great distress.
 One morning he threw the street door wide
On coming in, and his vigorous stride
Made the tools on his table rattle and jump.
In his hands he carried a new-burst clump
Of laurel blossoms, whose smooth-barked stalks
Were pliant with sap. As a husband talks
To the wife he left an hour ago,
Paul spoke to the Shadow. "Dear, you know
To-day the calendar calls it Spring,
And I woke this morning gathering
Asphodels, in my dreams, for you.
So I rushed out to see what flowers blew
Their pink-and-purple-scented souls
Across the town-wind's dusty scrolls,
And made the approach to the Market Square
A garden with smells and sunny air.
I feel so well and happy to-day,
I think I shall take a Holiday.
And to-night we will have a little treat.
I am going to bring you something to eat!"
He looked at the Shadow anxiously.
It was quite grave and silent. He
Shut the outer door and came

And leant against the window-frame.
"Dearest," he said, "we live apart
Although I bear you in my heart.
We look out each from a different world.
At any moment we may be hurled
Asunder. They follow their orbits, we
Obey their laws entirely.
Now you must come, or I go there,
Unless we are willing to live the flare
Of a lighted instant and have it gone."
A bee in the laurels began to drone.
A loosened petal fluttered prone.
"Man grows by eating, if you eat
You will be filled with our life, sweet
Will be our planet in your mouth.
If not, I must parch in death's wide drouth
Until I gain to where you are,
And give you myself in whatever star
May happen. O You Beloved of Me!
Is it not ordered cleverly?"
The Shadow, bloomed like a plum, and clear,
Hung in the sunlight. It did not hear.
 Paul slipped away as the dusk began
To dim the little shop. He ran
To the nearest inn, and chose with care
As much as his thin purse could bear.
As rapt-souled monks watch over the baking
Of the sacred wafer, and through the making
Of the holy wine whisper secret prayers
That God will bless this labour of theirs;
So Paul, in a sober ecstasy,
Purchased the best which he could buy.
Returning, he brushed his tools aside,
And laid across the table a wide napkin.
He put a glass and plate

On either side, in duplicate.
Over the lady's, excellent
With loveliness, the laurels bent.
In the centre the white-flaked pastry stood,
And beside it the wine flask. Red as blood
Was the wine which should bring the lustihood
Of human life to his lady's veins.
When all was ready, all which pertains
To a simple meal was there, with eyes
Lit by the joy of his great emprise,
He reverently bade her come,
And forsake for him her distant home.
He put meat on her plate and filled her glass,
And waited what should come to pass.
The Shadow lay quietly on the wall.
From the street outside came a watchman's call
"A cloudy night. Rain beginning to fall."
And still he waited. The clock's slow tick
Knocked on the silence. Paul turned sick.
He filled his own glass full of wine;
From his pocket he took a paper. The twine
Was knotted, and he searched a knife
From his jumbled tools. The cord of life
Snapped as he cut the little string.
He knew that he must do the thing
He feared. He shook powder into the wine,
And holding it up so the candle's shine
Sparked a ruby through its heart,
He drank it. "Dear, never apart
Again! You have said it was mine to do.
It is done, and I am come to you!"
 Paul Jannes let the empty wine-glass fall,
And held out his arms. The insentient wall
Stared down at him with its cold, white glare
Unstained! The Shadow was not there!

Paul clutched and tore at his tightening throat.
He felt the veins in his body bloat,
And the hot blood run like fire and stones
Along the sides of his cracking bones.
But he laughed as he staggered towards the door,
And he laughed aloud as he sank on the floor.

The Coroner took the body away,
And the watches were sold that Saturday.
The Auctioneer said one could seldom buy

Such watches, and the prices were high.

Madonna of the Evening Flowers

All day long I have been working,
Now I am tired. I call: "Where are you?"
But there is only the oak tree rustling in the wind.
The house is very quiet,
The sun shines in on your books,
On your scissors and thimble just put down,
But you are not there.
Suddenly I am lonely: Where are you?
I go about searching.
Then I see you,
Standing under a spire of pale blue larkspur,
With a basket of roses on your arm.
You are cool, like silver,
And you smile.
I think the Canterbury bells are playing little tunes.
You tell me that the peonies need spraying,
That the columbines have overrun all bounds,
That the pyrus japonica should be cut back and rounded.
You tell me these things.
But I look at you, heart of silver,
White heart-flame of polished silver,
Burning beneath the blue steeples of the larkspur.
And I long to kneel instantly at your feet,
While all about us peal the loud, sweet `Te Deums' of the Canterbury bells.

White and Green

Hey! My daffodil-crowned,
Slim and without sandals!
As the sudden spurt of flame upon darkness
So my eyeballs are startled with you,
Supple-limbed youth among the fruit-trees,
Light runner through tasselled orchards.
You are an almond flower unsheathed
Leaping and flickering between the budded branches.

Patterns

I walk down the garden paths,
And all the daffodils
Are blowing, and the bright blue squills.
I walk down the patterned garden-paths
In my stiff, brocaded gown.
With my powdered hair and jewelled fan,
I too am a rare
Pattern. As I wander down
The garden paths.

My dress is richly figured,
And the train
Makes a pink and silver stain
On the gravel, and the thrift
Of the borders.
Just a plate of current fashion,
Tripping by in high-heeled, ribboned shoes.
Not a softness anywhere about me,
Only whalebone and brocade.
And I sink on a seat in the shade
Of a lime tree. For my passion
Wars against the stiff brocade.
The daffodils and squills
Flutter in the breeze
As they please.
And I weep;
For the lime-tree is in blossom
And one small flower has dropped upon my bosom.

And the plashing of waterdrops
In the marble fountain
Comes down the garden-paths.
The dripping never stops.

Underneath my stiffened gown
Is the softness of a woman bathing in a marble basin,
A basin in the midst of hedges grown
So thick, she cannot see her lover hiding,
But she guesses he is near,
And the sliding of the water
Seems the stroking of a dear
Hand upon her.
What is Summer in a fine brocaded gown!
I should like to see it lying in a heap upon the ground.
All the pink and silver crumpled up on the ground.
I would be the pink and silver as I ran along the paths,
And he would stumble after,
Bewildered by my laughter.
I should see the sun flashing from his sword-hilt and the buckles
on his shoes.
I would choose
To lead him in a maze along the patterned paths,
A bright and laughing maze for my heavy-booted lover,
Till he caught me in the shade,
And the buttons of his waistcoat bruised my body as he clasped me,
Aching, melting, unafraid.
With the shadows of the leaves and the sundrops,
And the plopping of the waterdrops,
All about us in the open afternoon --
I am very like to swoon
With the weight of this brocade,
For the sun sifts through the shade.
Underneath the fallen blossom
In my bosom,
Is a letter I have hid.
It was brought to me this morning by a rider from the Duke.
"Madam, we regret to inform you that Lord Hartwell

Died in action Thursday se'nnight."
As I read it in the white, morning sunlight,
The letters squirmed like snakes.
"Any answer, Madam," said my footman.
"No," I told him.
"See that the messenger takes some refreshment.
No, no answer."
And I walked into the garden,
Up and down the patterned paths,
In my stiff, correct brocade.
The blue and yellow flowers stood up proudly in the sun,
Each one.
I stood upright too,
Held rigid to the pattern
By the stiffness of my gown.
Up and down I walked,
Up and down.
In a month he would have been my husband.
In a month, here, underneath this lime,
We would have broke the pattern;
He for me, and I for him,
He as Colonel, I as Lady,
On this shady seat.
He had a whim
That sunlight carried blessing.
And I answered, "It shall be as you have said."
Now he is dead.

In Summer and in Winter I shall walk
Up and down
The patterned garden-paths
In my stiff, brocaded gown.
The squills and daffodils
Will give place to pillared roses, and to asters, and to snow.
I shall go

Up and down,
In my gown.
Gorgeously arrayed,
Boned and stayed.
And the softness of my body will be guarded from embrace
By each button, hook, and lace.
For the man who should loose me is dead,
Fighting with the Duke in Flanders,
In a pattern called a war.
Christ! What are patterns for?

Lightning Source UK Ltd.
Milton Keynes UK
UKOW051022150713

213809UK00001B/25/P